HOW TO PLAN A SUSTAINABLE EVENT

More Books by Julia L Wright

Discover Essential Oils for Optimum Health

Lessons From Past Floods: *Destruction, Restoration and Preparation*

As A Man Thinketh by James Allen
Revised and enhanced by Julia L Wright

**Natural Health Book Series Based on
Orison Swett Marden's "Cheerfulness As A Life Power"**
Available on Kindle, revised and enhanced by Julia L Wright

Book 1: Laughter and Essential Oils:
Natural Cures for Dis-Ease

Book 2: Optimism and Essential Oils:
Natural Cures for Depression

Book 3: Positive Attitude and Essential Oils:
Natural Ways to Alleviate Stress

Book 4: Cheerfulness and Essential Oils:
Natural Ways to Create a Joyful Life

Book 5: Giving and Essential Oils:
Naturally Create the Life You Desire

Book 6: A Sunny Nature and Essential Oils:
Naturally Create Optimum Health

Books Published by HieroGraphics Books LLC

Handbook To Health **by Vivian Rice and Edie Wogaman**
Revised and edited by Julia L Wright

***Galloping Wind: The Legend of Wild Shadow, The Wind-That-Gallops*
by Zoltan Malocsay**

Where Do I Belong? **by Susan Grace**

Food Allergy Report - *Available on Kindle*
Edited by Julia L Wright

Children's Books Revised and Illustrated
by Julia Brown Wright
The Enchanted White Peacock
The Lost Rose Topaz Ring
The Last Dragon

HOW TO PLAN A SUSTAINABLE EVENT

A Guide For Creating A Waste Wise Event

Julia L Wright

****
HieroGraphics Books LLC

©2014 HieroGraphics Books LLC
All Rights Reserved
No Unauthorized Copying,
Editing or Distribution

Photographic Images by *Julia L. Wright* ©2014
Cover Design by HieroGraphics ©2014

Terms of Use and Disclaimer:
   No part of this book may be reproduced in whole or in part, or stored in a retrieval system or transmitted in any form or by any means electronic, recording, mechanical, photocopying or otherwise, without written permission of the publisher, except in the case of brief quotations embodied in critical articles or reviews.
   The Author and Publisher has strived to be as accurate and complete as possible in the creation of this book, notwithstanding the fact that due to due to the rapidly changing nature of the climate conditions and information she does not warrant or represent at any time that the all the contents within are still accurate. While all attempts have been made to verify information provided in this publication, the Author and Publisher assume no responsibility of liability for errors, omissions, or contrary interpretation of the subject matter herein.
   Any perceived slights of specific persons, peoples, or organizations are unintentional. The information presented in this book represents the view of the author as of the date of publication, the author reserves the right to alter and update opinions and information based upon new conditions and research.
   This book is presented for informational purposes only.

For information regarding permission, write to:
info@hierographicsbooksllc.com
Manitou Springs, CO

**Printed in the United States of America
First Printing, September 2014**

This book could not have been written without the support of the many individuals who have volunteered their time to help make Commonwheel Artists Annual Labor Day Art Festival more sustainable and contributed to this book.

I would particularly like to thank:
Alicia Archibald
Becky Elder
Brian Fritz
Kelly Snyder
Despina Struck
Kathleen Kelly
Councilwoman Coreen Toll
Councilwoman Nicole Nicolleta
Members of Transition Town Manitou Springs
Tricia Edwards and all the Zebulon Pike Boys
The many community volunteers who picked through the waste items to send them to their proper destinations.

Table Of Contents

Introduction	1
How This Book Came To Be Written	2
Chapter 1: What Is A Sustainable Event Or Festival?	5
Defining Sustainability	6
Sustainability Is Also A Call To Action	7
Dictionary Definitions Of Sustainable	8
Chapter 2: Why Create A Sustainable Event Or Festival?	9
A Sustainable Event Is Welcome In Any Community	10
Sustainable Events Make A Difference	11
Slowly Habits Are Changing	11
Events Are The Perfect Place to Start Implementing Sustainability	12
Enhance Your Organization's Positive Image	13
Save Money	14
Chapter 3: Necessary Components For A Sustainable Event Or Festival	17
Measuring Sustainable Success	18
A Different Type Of Volunteerism	19
Chapter 4: Waste Management	21
Proper Waste Management Is The Key Element For A Successful Sustainable Event	21
Sanitation Concerns At Outdoor Events	22
Limit Paper Use	23
Material Use And Distribution	24
Event Supplies	25
The Presenters	25
Lodging Options	25
Giveaways	26
Participant And Vendor Displays	27
Powering The Stage	28
Food And Beverage Service	29
Things To Consider When Choosing A Venue	30
Write Sustainable Language Into Your Venue Contract.	33

Chapter 5: Why Recycle? — 35
Some Interesting Facts About Recycling — 35
What happens To Recyclables? — 36
8 Major Benefits Of Recycling — 37
#1. Landfilling Is NOT A Sustainable Approach To A Healthy Environment. — 37
#2 Recycling Helps Prevent Pollution. — 38
#3 Recycling Reduces Worldwide Climate Changes. — 39
#4 Recycling Saves Our Natural Resources And Protects Wildlife. — 39
#5 Recycling Is Good For The Economy — 40
#6 Recycling Saves Money — 40
#7 Recycling Saves Energy — 41
#8 Recycling Is Easy To Do! — 41

Chapter 6: Why Collect And Compost Food Waste? — 43
Bioplastics — 43
Composting Creates By-Products That Can Be Used To Improve Soil — 44
Almost All Food Items Can Be Composted — 45
Compostable Food Service Products — 46
Items That Cannot Be Composted — 47
Exceptions — 47
The Best Way To Handle Liquid Waste — 48

Chapter 7: Case Study-Prime Example Of How To Create A Sustainable Festival — 49
Commonwheel Artists Annual Labor Day Art Festival As A Case Study — 49

Chapter 8: What Level of Sustainability Is The Goal For Your Event? — 53
Setting Goals — 53
Action Plan — 53
Share Your Goals And Plan — 54
How Will You Measure Your Success? — 55

Chapter 9: What All The Vendors Need To Know — 57
Getting Started — 57
During The Event — 58
Ways To Engage All Of Your Vendors, Not Just Food Vendors — 58
Announce Your Success — 59
Event In Review — 59

Chapter 10: Food Vendors Are Key Players At A Sustainable Event   **61**
Create Clear Guidelines   *62*
Eco-Friendly Serving Products   *63*
Food Packaging Ideas   *64*
Food Service Concerns For Indoor Or Catered Events   *64*

Chapter 11: Waste Collection And Disposal   **67**
Waste Collection Stations   *67*
Where To Locate Waste Collection Stations   *69*
Check And Recheck Again   *70*
Collection Bins   *70*
Liquid Waste   *72*
Grease   *73*
Human Waste   *73*
End Of Day Vigilance   *74*
A Short Cautionary Tale.   *75*
Items That Must Go To The Landfill   *75*

Chapter 12: Volunteers Needed   **77**
Where To Find Volunteers   *77*
Scheduling And Contact Information For Volunteers   *80*
Train Your Volunteers Well!   *82*
Job Related Items Waste Management Volunteers Will Need   *83*
How To "Reward" Your Volunteers   *84*

Chapter 13: Signage   **87**
Types Of Signs Needed   *87*
Printed Programs   *88*
No Programs Are Used At The Commonwheel Art Festival   *88*

Chapter 14: Press Releases Before and After the Event   **91**
Before The Event   *91*
Evaluation After The Event By Participants   *93*
After the Event Evaluate Measurable Successes   *94*
Celebrate Your Success!   *95*
Express Gratitude   *96*

Chapter 15: Lessons Learned — 99
Pictorial Signage Works Best — 99
Waste Monitor Duties — 99
Waste Containers — 100
Rogue Waste Containers — 101
Special Consideration For Food Vendors' Needs — 101
End Of Day Caveat — 102
Wildlife And Compost Or Any Food Waste — 103
Disposing Of Compostable Items — 104
It Gets Easier And Better Every Year — 104

Chapter 16: Emails, Letters And Facebook Posts — 105
Sample Letters — 105
Invitation To Volunteers — 106
Letters To Accepted Food Vendors And Participants If Not Forewarned — 108
Letters to Accepted Food Vendors And Participants If Forewarned — 108
Thank You Letters — 109
Success Announcements — 110

Chapter 17: Resources — 111
Recyclable And Compostable Service Ware — 112
Sustainable Lodging. — 113
Eco-Labeling — 113
Sustainable Organizations And Informative Websites — 113
Earth Friendly Promotional Products — 114
Solar Stages — 115
Where To Find Volunteers — 116
Sample Letters — 116
More information On Sustainability — 116

Chapter 18: In Conclusion — 117

About The Author — 123

Notes — 127

This book is dedicated to everyone who takes the time to compost, recycle, and reuse items so that they do not end by filling up landfills around the world.

Introduction

Creating a more sustainable event or festival should be the goal of every event organizer and festival coordinator.

It doesn't matter the size, or type of venue the event or festival will be held at, there are a variety of ways to make any event more eco-friendly, Waste Wise and sustainable.

Creating a sustainable event or festival takes vision and commitment from the organizing group and individuals within that organization.

Any type of event or festival can be both very successful and more sustainable with a minimum amount of effort.

Indoor events will have some challenges and requirements that are different from ones that need to be met for an outdoor festival. And the reverse is also true.

One can aim towards having a Waste-Free event or festival, but that is a very difficult goal to achieve. But creating a Waste Wise event is an attainable goal for any organizer when you implement even one of the strategies found inside this book. There are many ways to ensure the most diversion of waste possible for any Event you are planning.

This book contains many strategies for ways to help organizers to get started. Even if you chose just one of the outlined strategies to implement for the event or festival you host this year, you can make a positive difference for our environment and planet. At the same time, you will be helping to educate more people on the importance of sustainability in their everyday lives.

After having the first small success at becoming a more Waste Wise festival or event, everyone that contributed to this change will experience a feeling of satisfaction for having taken a step towards creating sustainability in his or her community. You are sure to find that everyone involved will have a suggestion or two on how the next event or festival can be even more sustainable. Many participants will feel inspired to implement another strategy or two in order to take the next step towards creating an even more sustainable event or festival in the following years.

Creating a sustainable event or festival has many benefits for your organization or business that go beyond just helping to conserve and restore the Earth's resources.

Using local presenters, entertainers or food sources not only benefits the ecosystem, but also has another advantage in that it supports your local economy.

When visitors and participants see these sustainable components suggested in this book in action at your event or festival, you know that you will also be educating them about the benefits of sustainability, and you can lead the way for change in your community.

Although the Commonwheel Artists Labor Day Art Festival was one of the first outdoor festivals in Colorado to actually require food vendors and participants to take steps that allowed for recycling and/or composting food waste, some of our food vendors had already been told they could not use Styrofoam products at other festivals and events. They could see that there would be more changes coming in the very near the future as municipalities were taking a closer look at how festivals and events impact the environment of the area they are held.

How This Book Came To Be Written

I, Julia Wright, have done a great deal of research on reasons for creating and ways to create more sustainable festivals and events.

In 2009, I started to put that research into action. With the help of many volunteers from the community, we have been able to continue with this concept of creating a more sustainable art festival in the following years at Commonwheel Artists Labor Day Weekend Art Festival.

In the near past, many people have called, or emailed to ask me about how to make their event or festival more sustainable. I found myself advising a variety of people with smaller events and indoor venues about how to make their event or festival more sustainable. I have mostly focused on how to handle waste at the Commonwheel Art Festival and in our gallery, but have researched many other concepts that would be useful for other festivals and events to implement.

After emailing many pieces of "paper" and trying to gather the information I thought would be helpful to each individual that inquired about this, I realized it would be far easier and more efficient to put all of this information into a book. This way I could help many small, or large organizations, everywhere create a sustainable and eco-friendly event or festival. These thoughtful inquiries inspired me to write this book to share the many insights I have gained these last few years working with community leaders, our city government, service providers and volunteers to create a more sustainable art festival.

My goal is to share this information with a larger audience to show how anyone can easily take a step or more towards making their festival or event more sustainable to become better stewards of his or her immediate environment and the Earth.

There is a lot of information available about creating a sustainable event, but it is scattered on many websites and books. Or, it is focused on very large events that have promoters with huge budgets and/or large corporations as sponsors.

My experience in creating a sustainable festival is based on a medium-sized outdoor art festival with a very small and extremely tight budget.

In 2009 Commonwheel Artists made its first attempt at being a more sustainable, Waste Wise art festival. Approximately 65% of the waste generated at that art festival was diverted from the local landfill.

This change in how we handled waste inspired some of our art patrons to volunteer the next year in order to help educate other attendees. Each year it has become a bit more sustainably successful.

After five (5) years of educating the art patrons who attended the art festival, it has become much easier for volunteers who sort through the waste collection bins to be sure that the different types of waste are disposed of in their proper containers.

In 2012, Commonwheel Artists Labor Day Weekend Art Festival was 80% Waste-Free.

In 2013, the Commonwheel Art Festival had to be relocated in just 3 weeks after the park it had been held in for the past 38 years was flooded on August 9, 2013. This caused many challenges for the organizer and some of them revolved around how to keep this festival as Waste Wise as possible.

The logistics for where the bins were placed wasn't perfect, and one mistake by a vendor bringing plastic ware that was not marked as compostable caused almost all of the plastic ware to become trash, rather than being composted.

That said, we still achieved a goal of diverting approximately 75% of the waste from the landfill and look forward to being even more successful as a Waste Wise Art Festival in the future.

Chapter 1

What Is A Sustainable Event Or Festival?

The most common definition of a sustainable event or festival is one that aims to have a minimal impact on the environment where it is held.

There are many ways this can be done.

Every eco-friendly piece an organization adds to its event or festival helps to decrease any harmful impact to the environment it had in past years.

Some people use the term "Green" event. That term seems a bit limiting for the complete definition, or whole idea, of what an organization can achieve when looking at the big picture of how any event impacts our environment, now and in the future.

In this book, I have chosen to use the concept of Sustainability to encompass the many ways you can create a *"eco-friendly"* or *"Green"* Sustainable event or festival.

In the following text, in most places the word Event with a capital E is meant to encompass all types of small and large festivals and events; *including art, food or music festivals, weddings, training workshops, conferences, seminars or any type of gathering together of many people that has been planned in advance.*

Organization planners for each type of sustainable Event are sure to have different goals and approaches to reach their optimum level of sustainability.

But each one will have one common goal. Every one of these organizations will be aiming to make a positive difference for the environment by adding the least amount of waste or pollution to the Earth as possible.

There are many components needed to create a sustainable Event. In this book you will find suggestions and guidelines anyone can use to create a more sustainable Event.

This book addresses the many levels of sustainability an organization might choose to have as a goal for its Event. It includes practical suggestions for a number of ways to reach the level of sustainability that is right for your Event.

Wouldn't NOW be a good time to start planning how to make your Event more sustainable?

Defining Sustainability

Since the 1980s, sustainability has been used mostly when discussing human sustainability on planet Earth.

The concept of *"sustainability"* is used to describe an economy that balances doing business in a way that is in balance with basic ecological support systems.

Sustainability relates to how long we can keep doing what we are doing without coming to an end of a resource that supports this action. It is about improving the quality of human life while living within the capacity of supporting ecosystems.

Sustainable means living and doing business in ways that use natural resources without using them all up or finding ways to replenish them. Healthy ecosystems and environments are necessary to the survival of humans and other organisms. Ways of reducing negative human impact means we must manage and protect environmental resources.

The term *"sustainable development"* rose to significance after it was used in 1987 in the Brundtland Commission report *Our Common Future.* (http://www.un-documents.net/wced-ocf.htm)

In this report, the commission coined what has become the most often-quoted definition of sustainable development: *"sustainable development is development that meets the needs of the present without compromising the ability of future generations to meet their own needs."* Sustainable development ties together concern for the carrying capacity of natural systems with the social, political, and economic challenges faced by humanity.

Sustainability Is Also A Call To Action

Moving towards sustainability is also a social challenge that must be addressed by urban planning and transport, local and individual lifestyles and ethical consumerism.

Sustainability requires actions that involve local and global efforts to meet basic human needs without destroying or degrading the natural environment.

Sustainability implies responsible and proactive decision-making and innovation that minimizes negative impact and maintains balance between ecological resilience, economic prosperity and cultural vibrancy to ensure a desirable planet for all species now and in the future.

Ways of living and doing business in sustainable ways can take many paths.

Creating a more sustainable event or festival is just one step in the right direction towards helping people make adjustments in their individual lifestyles that will help to conserve natural resources.

Organizers that are looking to create a more sustainable festival or event often attempt to reduce their carbon footprint by altering methods of handling waste, food service, water consumption, information distribution, cleaning, energy use, and/or transportation.

Sustainability in business must address the concepts of ecological economics by using a multidimensional perspective when addressing environmental and ecological variables and issues. Creating sustainability must integrate the concepts of public welfare and conserving natural resources in ways that create viable profit margins. Social, cultural, health-related and financial aspects have to be integrated into the analysis to create a situation that is viable on all levels. To do this, we must use strategies and technology that finds ways to encourage economic growth while limiting environmental damage and resource depletion.

Dictionary Definitions Of Sustainable

sus·tain·a·ble [suh-stey-nuh-buhl] adjective
1. capable of being sustained.
2. capable of being supported or upheld, as by having its weight borne from below.
3. pertaining to a system that maintains its own viability by using techniques that allow for continual reuse.
4. capable of being maintained at a steady level without exhausting natural resources or causing severe ecological damage: sustainable development.
5. able to be maintained or kept going, as an action or process: a sustainable negotiation between the two countries.
6. able to be confirmed or upheld: a sustainable decision.
7. able to be supported as with the basic necessities or sufficient funds: a sustainable life.

A simple definition of sustainability *is improving the quality of human life while living within the capacity of supporting ecosystems.*

Sustainability involves the defining of a set of actions to be taken by humans that will not diminish the prospects of future generations to enjoy similar levels of health, consumption, wealth, utility, or welfare comparable to those enjoyed by those currently living on Earth.

More information about sustainability can be found at: http://en.wikipedia.org/wiki/Sustainability

Chapter 2

Why Create A Sustainable Event Or Festival?

In this chapter you can explore some of the many reasons it would be wise to create a sustainable event or festival.

Listed below are some concepts that will resonate with almost anyone who has ever organized an Event.
1. By holding a more sustainable Event, individuals and organizations have the opportunity to have a very positive affect on our Earth's environment and give future generations a cleaner and more beautiful World by doing so.
2. Events are usually held at a centralized location, which makes it easier to collect, and then divert waste away from the landfill and be repurposed into useful products.
3. When many people work together towards a common goal, it helps to create a sense of community. In this type of positive thinking atmosphere, ideas abound on how to accomplish this goal.
4. At large Events, hundreds or thousands of people are gathered together that can be educated about what items can be recycled or composted and diverted from the landfill. They can take this knowledge home with them and put it to use in their daily lives.
5. Other event organizers will be inspired to follow your lead when they see your success and hear people talking about your positive impact on the environment.

6. Everyone in your organization will feel good about taking action and making some changes that future generations will appreciate.
7. More and more municipalities are seeing sustainability as an important factor when considering an Event's impact on their city.

A Sustainable Event Is Welcome In Any Community

As environmental issues become more important to an ever increasing segment of the public, demand for appropriate practices regarding how waste is handled at Events will increase.

More and more municipalities are seeing sustainability as an important factor when considering an Event and the impact it can have on their city when a large number of visitors gather in one location on a specific date. Some have already started requiring a plan from Event organizers to describe how they intend to handle the large amounts of waste that will be generated at their Event.

In the past, most sustainable Events have been created by a group of environmentally aware people who are focused on creating a healthy planet for future generations. These people have stepped to work together and invested the extra effort involved in various projects to create a healthier environment and a more sustainable economy in other ways than just creating a sustainable Event.

They often start in small ways. Then when others joined in, or they are applauded their efforts, their vision gained momentum and the support of the community. In a very short time, they discovered they had proven in many ways that small changes in waste handling that could have a huge positive impact on the people who attend their Event and the city where it takes place.

When you look at how intertwined everything is: the environment, economic benefits, a balanced community and public education, you discover even more reasons to take the steps to create a more sustainable Event when planning your next Event.

Sustainable Events Make A Difference

For every ounce of waste that is diverted from a landfill, it is one less piece of trash that will be totally wasted rather than reused in some form or another. When a recycled item is used to create a new product it means one less piece of newly mined material to be dug from the earth or one less tree that needs to be cut down to create this product. That is a big win for the Earth and future generations.

If we continue to stay on the same path for handling waste as we currently do, and nothing changes, we are creating an unsustainable situation. Future generations that will need to cope with what we are doing to the Earth will wonder why we did not have the forethought to be better stewards of the world we were living in so they could enjoy a healthy environment also.

Having a vision for creating a more sustainable Event is just the beginning for creating a more sustainable Future for everyone.

Having the courage to implement even one of these steps at your Event means that you are taking a step towards making positive change for all of our Futures.

Slowly Habits Are Changing.

Slowly, a movement towards creating a more sustainable World has taken hold in many places and in a variety of ways.

Al Gore's Oscar winning documentary *"An Inconvenient Truth"* started many conversations around the country. Many people and businesses began to consider the impact of sending everything to the landfill when he or she finished using it, rather than giving it a new useful life.

Some visionary business owners began looking at *"greener"* ways to run their company.

Many individuals began to take small steps to learn how to make their own worlds more sustainable.

Recycling has become much more mainstream.

Reusable bags have become fashionable and a statement about a person's concern for the environment.

People started exploring the idea of composting and creating small gardens in places they never considered planting fruits or vegetables before.

People everywhere began to take a closer look at what we were doing to our air, water and soil. Many discovered that if they could change one, or many habits, they could help keep those life-giving sources from being poisoned and safe for future generations to enjoy.

Events Are The Perfect Place To Start Implementing Sustainability

Isn't it time that you consider your Event's carbon footprint as you plan it this coming year?

Although it is very difficult to reach a Zero-Waste Event goal, it should not stop an organization or event coordinator from doing the best they possibly can to reduce the impact of their Event has on the environment by creating a Waste Wise Event.

Creating a Waste Wise Event is a much easier goal to aim for as you plan ways to make your next Event a more sustainable Event.

Every Event where large numbers of people come together creates a huge amount of waste that is gathered in one area, and in the past, has all just been sent to a landfill.

Many festival and event organizers have started to look at what they could do in small or large ways to divert waste items from being sent to our quickly filling and pollution creating landfills.

Recycling certain items is about the easiest sustainable component to add to any Event.

Adding a recycling component to any Event will help keep tons of materials out of the landfill that can become useful products again.

Composting is a bit more challenging, but is the biggest environmental win.

The Earth gets back healthy soil from various items. Food items, which would have just been "wasted" are easily composted. Uneaten food, compostable paper products and corn-based utensils can become useful instead of taking up space in a landfill where they create methane gas as they waste away. Instead, when composted, they are able to give back much-needed minerals to help replenish the Earth they came from originally.

Another simple step, especially at indoor events, you can offer a Water Station instead handing out hundreds of water bottled in plastic containers. Invite attendees to bring their own water containers and have free refills available. Or have a give away water bottle with your logo imprinted on it for them to use in the future and advertise how you created a more sustainable Event.

Another goal would be to use less energy at the event. Devising ways to use less power, or having an alternative energy source of energy would be a big win for any Event.

Having more energy efficient sources of transportation to get participants to the Event can have a huge impact on lowering your event's carbon footprint. Offering a reward to those who travel there using public transportation, carpooling, on a bike or by foot can inspire people to rethink the way they travel to local Events. These actions help divert pollution from the air we breathe.

There are many more suggestions in this book of ways to create a more sustainable event, but these a few great ideas to consider where your might want to start.

Event organizers are invited to use this book as a guide to make find ideas and ways to make one or more change in various areas of your Event to create a more sustainable Event.

Enhance Your Organization's Positive Image

Creating a sustainable Event will help to build your reputation as an environmentally conscious organization.

Exhibiting environmental stewardship makes you business more interesting and the Event will seem a better place to volunteer when someone is considering ways to give back to their community.

Branding your Event as a "Sustainable" Event will open up dialogue in your community. You can put this fact in your advertising and share it using Social Media to be sure you reap the benefits of being seen as an organization that is doing the right thing.

Attendees will notice the measures you have taken to minimize your Event's environmental impact and they will remember your Event in very positive ways as being different from other similar Events they might consider attending.

Many municipalities have created awards that honor and support individuals, businesses or organizations that are involved in creating a more sustainable Earth. They usually announce these awards in a press release, and/or at an awards ceremony that will give your Event an extra publicity boost in your community. Receiving public recognition of an Event's success as a sustainable Event can be used to promote your Event in Press Releases, posts on Facebook or in an email when inviting the public to your Event the following year.

Save Money

Making your Event, or even business meetings, more sustainable can be very cost effective for your organization.

Waste is a major expense to any Event's budget. Cutting down on waste will help your bottom line look greener.

Did you know that having condiments available in larger containers, rather than using individual packets could save you about 50% on your condiment expenditure?

Consider having a water station instead handing out plastic bottles of individual servings of water to save the organization money and avoid waste.

Always be sure you buy items in bulk quantities when possible. Large packets of napkins, paper towels and toilet paper saves on packing materials, are easier to store. Making bulk purchases can save a lot of money for these types of purchases.

Once you start thinking about how your large or small Event can be more sustainable, you will find many ways that it also will save your organization money.

Chapter 3

Necessary Components For A Sustainable Event Or Festival

There are many factors to consider when creating a sustainable Event or Festival.

Below are some of the major factors to consider as you begin to plan for a more sustainable Event.

- Goals must be carefully outlined for a sustainable Event.
- A plan needs to be set in place for handling waste differently than it has been handled in the past.
- Volunteers are a key factor in creating a successful sustainable event. It is necessary to determine how many will be needed and where they will be found.
- The venue must be researched to determine how easy, or difficult, it will be to create a sustainable Event at this location.
- Vetting all service providers must be handled a bit differently. You will need to ask them about what *"green"* or sustainable practices currently employ. It will be important to explain to them the goal of the sustainable Event and ways they are expected to help reach that goal.
- Guidelines for all types of participants must be created and clearly communicated to them.
- Ways to measure the success of the Event needs to be set in place in before the Event is scheduled to take place.

In this book you will find strategies to address the above, and many more issues.

Measuring Sustainable Success

It is important to measure different factors to see how successful your sustainable Event efforts were each year.

One of the most common measurements of success is to determine how much waste was diverted from the landfill.

Events need a way to look at the Waste Diversion percentage. This is determined by how much of the total waste that is generated at an Event actually ends up in a landfill compared to how much goes to a recycling and/or a composting facility.

If one company handles all the waste, they usually have ways of weighing it at their facility to calculate these percentages.

More often, the organizer must look at the amount of waste waiting to be hauled away in the various types of containers. Then they must estimate based on the size of containers and how full they are, the percentages going to each type of facility.

A goal to aim for would be to divert 80% of the waste generated at the Event away from a landfill. That probably won't happen in your first year, or even the next few years. But even a 25% diversion should be considered a huge win!

The amount of waste that can be diverted from the landfill is dependent upon many factors.

The size, location and type of venue that an Event is held at plays a huge part in how sustainable an Event can be.

An important piece is making sure all the vendors, as well as the attendees, are aware of the programs they need to participate in to make the Event as sustainable as possible.

The types of items used for serving food and beverages play a huge part in creating a sustainable Event. As many disposable items as possible should be either recyclable or compostable.

If you are only integrating recycling, and not composting, into your waste management plan, as many food service items as possible need to be recyclable.

Sadly, any paper item, such as plates or napkins that has food on it cannot be recycled. But most plastic cups that have been used to serve liquids in can be recycled. Although ones used for smoothies and milk shakes, or similar products, don't fit in the recyclable category.

If using a Water Station, keep track of how many gallons of water are given away. This can help you calculate how many plastic water bottles were not used.

Straws cannot be recycled. There are straws that are made out of compostable material, but there is no such thing as a recyclable straw. Ask vendors to only offer straws when absolutely necessary if composting is not offered at the Event.

Whether you employ one or both types of services, you need to give very detailed instructions to food vendors regarding what they can use for serving food items at the event.

A Different Type Of Volunteerism

Volunteers are an important component to having most Events run smoothly.

A sustainable event or festival requires a whole other level of enthusiasm and commitment from its volunteers to make it as successful as possible.

It does take extra hands and committed volunteers to get this job done properly. Sorting all the waste properly takes extra time and effort, but in the long run it is well worth it.

Fortunately, finding eco-minded individuals is pretty easy these days.

Many Events offer volunteers free access to the Event in trade for a specific number of hours they work. If that doesn't work for your Event, it would be beneficial to offer some type of reward that fits in with the sustainable vision. *(See chapter 12)*

Chapter 4

Waste Management

Whether volunteers or paid staff handles your waste management, how they are trained will have a huge effect on the ultimate outcome of everyone's efforts to create the most sustainable Event possible.

Having very clear visual aids (graphics) for your volunteers or staff, and the public will make the sorting and disposing of waste items much easier for everyone involved.

Proper Waste Management Is The Key Element For A Successful Sustainable Event

An Event's waste management plan must include providing recycling and/or composting receptacles located near all trash bins.

Separate, well labeled, receptacles for all types of waste stream items created at the event or festival must be placed very close to each other. This will make it easier for attendees and participants to discern where to dispose of the waste they have in their hands.

Be sure all the receptacles are well marked and have signage or has graphic images that clearly defines what type of waste is to be disposed of in each type of available waste receptacles.

It can be very helpful to have volunteers stationed at the waste receptacles to assist participants placing their waste items in the correct receptacles. *"Bin Guardians"* or *"Recycling Monitors"* or *"Waste Rustlers"* can help educate people about why your event is making this effort and start conversations about the value of being a sustainable Event.

If you can't have volunteers stationed at all the waste areas, it is important to have them monitor the waste receptacles at regular intervals. This assures that they can sort out improperly placed waste items before each receptacle is taken to the final collection bins to avoid contamination.

Sanitation Concerns At Outdoor Events

Hiring an eco-conscious portable restroom company is another way to lower your Event's impact on the environment.

Many portable restroom companies currently are becoming more eco-friendly in many ways.

Make sure you inquire about how eco-friendly the various components they use in their units when hiring a portable restroom company for any outdoor festival or any other type of event.

Many of these types of companies now use biodegradable solutions in the waste tanks, rather than the harsh, powerful smelling chemicals that were the standard in the past. Look for a portable restroom company that uses a 100% biodegradable solution to break down the waste and controls the odor in the waste tanks. Be sure they can guarantee that this solution is formaldehyde free, contains no petrochemicals, has not been tested on animals and will not harm the environment, plant or animal life.

All the cleaning products they will be using also need to be biodegradable, formaldehyde-free, contain no petrochemicals and have not been tested on animals.

You will want to be assured the anti-bacterial hand gel sanitizer is biodegradable, formaldehyde free, contains no parabens and is made from renewable resources.

Requesting these guarantees will assure you, and your attendees, the components used in all of their products are safe to touch and breathe.

You will also want to find out if they use recycled paper products. Toilet paper should meet EPA certified procurement guidelines. That means they have a minimum of 95% recycled content of which 20% is post consumer and has 95% less packaging waste than standard roll toilet paper. Both the core and packaging should be made from recycled paper and be recyclable.

Paper towels should also meet EPA certified procurement guidelines, which is a little different from the toilet paper guidelines. They should have a minimum 95% recycled content of which 50% is post consumer.

Bulk packaging is another way to have less negative impact on the environment. Portable restroom companies have the opportunity to buy all items needed to service and be used by the public in bulk with very little packaging.

Limit Paper Use

Technology keeps evolving new ways to help Event organizers to avoid needing to use as much paper as in the past. Using emails, websites, Facebook pages and other options can be very helpful.

You will want to look for ways to provide as much Event information (advertisements, invitations, announcements, instructions, etc.) via electronic means as feasible.

Facebook, websites and email lists are paramount to creating a successful Event or Festival. Use these tools as efficiently and effectively as possible for sharing information with all types of participants and the public.

Facebook, Twitter and blog posts on a website tied to the Event can save some of the cost of advertising. Social Media often is more effective than print ads. Slowly mix in Social Media ads with other successful advertising campaigns you have used in the past. Be sure to get emails from as many attendees as possible for future Events.

Many types of Events and Festivals can offer online registration options.

For some Events, SmartPhones and tablets can be used to show proof of registration that was emailed to the attendee or participant. Displaying this proof of registration on a SmartPhone or tablet can then be verified on a computer at the registration desk.

Many Events have name badges for attendees. Paper name badges can be placed in a recycle bin at the exit.

Plastic badges that the paper name tags are inserted into can be re-used many times over. Make it easy for participant to recycle them at the end of the event by providing collection baskets at all exits from the event.

Be sure that the paper name tags are printed on paper that has a high recycled content. Although the paper name card that is inside a plastic badge may not be reusable, the paper it is printed upon can be recycled.

Material Use And Distribution

It would be important to request that presenters use a very limited number of paper handouts at any Event. Suggest to presenters and vendors that they pass out printed materials to participants only when absolutely necessary.

Conferences, performance trainings, educational workshops and seminars, are most usually held at indoor venues that often have a large amount of informational materials the presenters and speakers want to share with their attendees.

When it is absolutely necessary to have paper handouts, ask presenters to make green choices. They can use recycled content paper (Chlorine free; 100% recycled content; 50% post-consumer fiber is the EPA standard.)

When making color copies be aware that goldenrod and fluorescent-colored paper is almost impossible to recycle.

Currently there are many print companies who use vegetable-based inks, which are more environmentally friendly than traditional inks. Creating a double-sided copy saves paper.

Be sure there are designated containers by all exits where attendees can recycle or return unwanted copies at the end of an Event.

An Event organizer can encourage participants to share their information by creating electronic copies of materials that attendees can access on their computers, tablets, SmartPhones, etc.

If one person or organization is doing the majority of the presenting, they can offer their information to attendees by providing them with a CD, DVD or USB drive and/or make their trainings or information available on their website.

If the conference or speaker is being recorded, these recordings can be placed on a website page that needs a password to access it after the conference ends.

Sometimes a speaker may want to put their talk on YouTube where others can find it as an introduction to a full course or training they may offer relating to the topic they spoke upon at the Event.

Event Supplies

When purchasing supplies for your Event, you will want to ask these questions:
- Is it really necessary?
- Can it be recycled?
- Can it be composted?
- Can it be repurposed and/or reused?
- Is there a similar item with a recycled content option?
- Can it be purchased with minimal packaging?
- Can it be bought in bulk with less packaging?
- Can it be reused at a future event or festival?

The Presenters

Do a search in your local or regional area to identify experts in your area to be presenters to help publicize local initiatives and talent.

Send out emails to your presenters and entertainers to gather information you need from them and explain your sustainable goals to them.

Request presenters to send electronic documents with their biographical material and photographs to be used in publicity releases and added to the Event's website.

Ask each presenter or entertainer to clearly define what their audio and visual requirements will be for their part in the Event.

When connecting with the presenters by email, be sure to ask if they have any specific dietary needs to make their time spent at the event as pleasant and as comfortable as possible.

Lodging Options

There is a national list of "green" hotels that can be used to select potential rooms for out-of-town participants.

Offer lodging that is close to the Event so that they can easily walk to it. Or, if the Event is held in a hotel, ask the hotel if they can offer a discounted rate for attendees and participants. Then encourage participants to stay at this location.

In some instances it may be appropriate to ask members of the organization or planning committee to act as host for presenters.

In the resource section you will find ways to located "green" hotels in the area your Event will be held.

Giveaways

Event organizers can suggest to all participants that their giveaway items can be consumed, used for a long time, and/or be recycled.

Many companies in the USA create items with a logo on it that an attendee has a need for, and they will be able to use many times in the future.

Suggested items listed below can easily have a business logo and contact information printed on them. Each time a participant uses one of these items, they see it and remember the company who gave it away in a positive way.

- Reusable bags
- Key chains
- Small flashlights
- Coffee mugs
- Reusable water bottles
- Note pads made from recycled content
- Pens and pencils
- T-shirts
- Magnets

There are too many types of items offered by a wide variety of companies to list here. Take some time and Google the type of item you want to use to find what best fits your Event and budget.

Some of these items work better than a business card because it won't get tossed in a Rolodex, never to surface again. But many of these items will get used up and the company's information will be tossed out with the container making it more difficult to find than a business card. So it depends on what message you are trying to share for these to work.

Below is a list of a few ideas for attention-getting items that I have recently seen at sustainable Events. They all had a company's logo and contact information printed on them.

- Handmade lip balm packaged with the organization's contact information printed on the same label as the ingredients.
- Seed Packets. A clever gardener collected seeds and printed a picture of the plant with growing information on one side and a company's name and contact information on the other side.
- A paper planter. It is a cleverly designed paper container that you can start an herb in, this one had basil, then transplant in a few weeks. The Business's name was displayed prominently on two sides. (Garden Gems)
- Salsa made by a local company printed a label with their contact information and the location of a restaurant serving meals using their brand of salsa.
- Honey from a local beekeeper had a label with their website telling where to find local markets where it is sold.
- A school offering programs for children gave away small cases with watercolors and a brush with their logo and contact information printed on a label on the top.
- A printed coupon or code that can be placed on an SmartPhone for a free drink or appetizer to participants who dine at specific restaurants located near the Event.

Get creative!

Connect with local artists, businesses or small food companies to create something that will be unique and useful to a participant long after the Event has ended.

Participant And Vendor Displays

Indoor Events can suggest that vendors use reusable and/or recycled/recyclable materials for their booths, displays, exhibits and/or in their presentations.

Indoor venues often have many of the items an exhibitor needs for a reasonable rental fee. Venues that have many Events where exhibitors sell products or consult with potential clients can usually supply tables and chairs and/or curtain dividers for free, or a small fee. Encourage exhibitors to take advantage of these types of items so they won't need to use large vehicles or rent trailers to bring these types of items from their business location. Needing to use a smaller vehicle will help them save on transportation costs and less pollution will be emitted into the atmosphere.

Powering The Stage

There are companies springing up all over the country offering a solar-powered stage option for powering stages at outdoor events and festivals.

Some are even willing to bring their stage for advertising at a small venue. Others will charge a fee related to how much power is used and relative to the cost that would have been charged by the power company to supply that amount of electricity.

Do some searches in your area to find out if such an option is available to your Event.

Food And Beverage Service

All events and festivals have the option to require all food service items used can be reused, recycled or composted, depending on your waste management plan.

Styrofoam serving containers must be banned from all events and festivals!

The type of serving items that can be used at indoor events greatly varies from what can be used at an outdoor festival. When dishwashing facilities are available at the venue it is a viable option for food to be served on plates using regular silverware. And, people can enjoy beverages using real glassware and coffee cups.

Indoor events should consider avoiding using single-serving containers for anything. Having larger containers for condiments, sugar, cream, etc., means less waste is generated. Some single serve items can be composted, such as sugar packets, but small single serving containers for condiments and cream cannot be recycled or reused.

At outdoor events and festivals, some, but not all food vendors can adopt a policy of not using single serving containers. It just isn't as easy to comply with this idea in an outdoor setting. Wind and weather conditions are important factors to consider at such Events. They can make it more difficult to keep large condiment items clean and on a table in away that they won't be blown off.

Conferences, seminars, performance trainings, information sharing classes and workshops may also be catered or have on-site food service options. If the Event is catered, it is necessary to talk with the caterer, or the on-site kitchen managers, about what types of meals they normally serve. Discuss with them what they could do to create more sustainable meals for the Event.

At Events where large groups of people will be gathered to eat meals, consider providing food "buffet-style" instead of using individually packaged "boxed" meals or pre-plated quantities. This saves on container waste and allows people to take only what they want to eat.

When choosing a food service vendor or caterer you will want to look for one who will support your sustainable Event decisions. For a sustainable Event, it is also important to discuss what their approach to recycling and/or composting is, and if they are willing to comply with your Event's guidelines to be as sustainable or *"green"* as possible.

When looking at the type of meals to be served, consider the possibility of using a food service provider or caterer who has a policy that includes purchasing food from locally available sources whenever feasible. When chefs, caterers or food service vendors use local produce it supports local farms and farmers, which in turn gives a boost to the local economy.

Be sure your food service provider or caterer can provide vegetarian or vegan options for participants. Ask them about gluten free options they might also be able to provide.

You might want to consider the possibility of serving only meatless meals at your event. This is a huge positive for the environment. If the Event has a compostable option, these types of meals would involve food scraps that are totally compostable, no extra sorting required.

Encourage participants to take excess food with them (in environmentally friendly packaging) and/or make arrangements to have excess food taken to local food banks or shelters.

Find out if they serve shade grown, organic, fair-trade certified coffee and teas. If not, would they please look into that as an option and let you know how much it would add to their fee.

Request they set-up water and beverage stations using reusable containers, such as pitchers or large water jugs with spigots, instead of offering individual glass or plastic bottles filled with water, teas or juices.

Ask them if they collect used cooking grease and have it collected to become biodiesel fuel? Many small companies are sprouting up around the country that offer this service. Do a search to see if one is available in the area of your venue and have that information ready to share with your food service provider or caterer.

In these changing times it is getting easier and easier to find food service vendors and caterers that have already made a commitment to sustainability. Ask the food service provider or caterer if they have a sustainability coordinator. You can request they share their environmental policy with you to see how well it fits your sustainable event guidelines.

You will want to be assured that the service provider has a recycling and/or composting strategy. If they do not, find out if will they be willing to work with a waste management system that is set up to handle recycling and/or composting at the event. Each sustainable Event organizer will want to contact the venue's waste management service to ensure all recyclable and compostable materials will be processed appropriately by service staff at the venue and when it reaches its end destination.

Things To Consider When Choosing A Venue

Choose a site that is near public transportation and/or consider providing shuttle service from centralized locations where many people can park or will be debarking from a train or bus. Pedal cab companies are springing up in many areas and are a fun way to travel from a motel to the Event's location. Remember to publicize all the transit options in the outreach materials sent to your participants and the public.

Research Event sites, contractors (organizers, caterers, etc.), and suppliers (paper, printers, bioware manufacturers, etc.) to be sure they have a commitment to sustainable practices.

Find out if your local area has a green services directory or a green business program. These are great resources to help create a more sustainable Event.

Some venues have already made a commitment to sustainability. Finding a venue that has made this type of commitment makes it much easier to reach the goals for a sustainable Event. Green Lodging News is a great source for finding a sustainable venue in your area. Or, Google "Sustainable Event Venues (your city's name)" and see what shows up in your area.

When choosing a venue for a sustainable Event, consider these questions:

- Will the venue support your green decisions?
- Does the venue have a sustainability coordinator?
- Does the venue have an environmental policy?
- What is the venue's recycling/composting strategy?
- Does the venue purchase carbon offsets?
- Does the venue have renewable energy on site?
- Does the venue use energy efficient lighting and appliances where possible?
- Will lights and air conditioning be turned off when rooms are not in use?
- If the venue does not use a waste management service that recycles/composts, will they allow you to bring in a service that will?

For small events or festivals, if there is no other option, you may have to handle the all of the recycling/composting yourself. The Commonwheel Art Festival handled the disposal of the compostable waste for two years with great success.

Write Sustainable Language Into Your Venue Contract.

The sustainable language that needs to be written into the venue contract will vary depending on the type of Event, venue and the Event's sustainable goal.

For example, include a statement in the venue contract to require the venue to commit to "minimizing the environmental impact of the [name of event] (the event)" by doing one, or all of the following actions:
- Decreasing the amount of solid waste produced by the Event.
- Reducing energy and water consumption at the Event.
- Minimizing or offsetting harmful emissions resulting from energy consumption associated with the Event.
- Disposing of solid and liquid waste in an environmentally responsible manner.
- Eliminating the use of harmful chemicals at or for the Event.

You may want to have a consultation with a lawyer to be sure you have written the contract in a way both parties will be clear about what is expected from the other, and the actions needed to be taken by everyone to fulfill the requirements set forth in the contract signed by both parties.

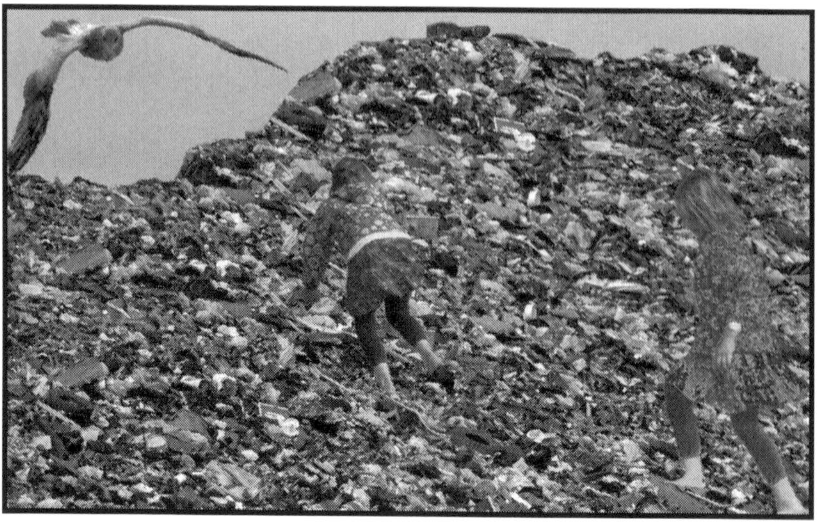

Chapter 5

Why Recycle?

To understand the value of recycling, we must look at the entire life cycle of a product. Start from the extraction and processing of raw materials, then the manufacturing process of the product and ending with its final disposal.

Recycling creates a closed-loop system where once used, now unwanted items are returned back to manufacturers for use in new products. This prevents the pollution and destruction that occurs when virgin materials like trees are harvested and precious metals are extracted from the earth.

Some Interesting Facts About Recycling

80% or more of the items we normally throw away could potentially be recovered through reuse, recycling or composting.

- Recycling is a daily activity for more than 100 million Americans. There are more Americans who recycle than vote.
- Recycling keeps useable items out of the landfill that can be transformed into new useful products.
- Paper products are easy to collect and recycle. It is valuable to recycle paper to save forests from being destroyed for a product that can be easily transformed into another use.
- Aluminum is also easy to collect and is infinitely recyclable. Aluminum can be repurposed many times. Each time it is recycled it can be used to create another new product that can often be recycled again.

- Many cities have adopted curbside recycling programs as standard waste management practices. There are over 9,000 curbside recycling programs in the USA, and that number is growing all the time.
- If you don't have the option to use a curbside recycling program you can take advantage of more than 12,000 drop-off centers around the country.
- A few communities currently recycle and compost at least 60% of their waste.
- It is a great way to protect our environment and stimulate our economy.

What Happens To Recyclables?

New products are created from things that are placed into recycling bins.
- Glass bottles become new glass bottles.
- Aluminum cans are turned back into aluminum cans, and can be recycled almost indefinitely.
- Steel cans are used in other steel products such as car parts and construction materials, and can also be recycled over and over again.
- Plastic bottles are recycled into carpet, clothing, auto parts, and new plastic bottles.
- Paper is recycled into new paper. Some grades of paper can be recycled up to seven times.

8 Major Benefits Of Recycling

By demonstrating what can be recycled and how easy it is to recycle at an Event, many more people will begin to recycle items at their homes. Thus by creating a more sustainable Event, there will be a chain reaction of more people taking actions that help create a more sustainable World.

There are many good reasons to recycle on a daily basis.

Below are 8 major reasons everyone should participate in recycling whenever possible.

1. **Landfilling is not a sustainable approach to a healthy environment.**
2. **Recycling helps prevent pollution.**
3. **Recycling reduces Worldwide Climate Changes.**
4. **Recycling saves our natural resources and protects wildlife.**
5. **Recycling is good for the economy.**
6. **Recycling saves money.**
7. **Recycling saves energy.**
8. **It's easy to do!**

#1. Landfilling Is NOT A Sustainable Approach To A Healthy Environment.

Recycling avoids the need for new landfills.

Roughly 20% of the sites on the Superfund list (the nation's most hazardous sites) are solid waste landfills. There are reports from the EPA that reveal the possibility all landfill liners will eventually leak and their toxic garbage liquids will seep into and contaminate soil and groundwater supplies under them.

When recycled materials go into new products, they don't go into landfills, so landfill space is conserved and fewer greenhouse gases are formed.

It is getting harder and harder to find new areas that will accept the type of waste landfills must accept. No one wants to live next to a landfill and the potential environmental hazards they bring with them.

#2. Recycling Helps Prevent Pollution.

Recycling supports public health by not adding toxins into the air we breathe, the water we drink and the earth that grows our foods.

When recycled materials are used in place of virgin materials during manufacturing, we avoid the environmental damage caused by mining for metals, drilling for petroleum, fracking for natural gas and harvesting trees.

Recycling and remanufacturing are much more effective in reducing greenhouse gas emissions than landfilling and virgin manufacturing.

Creating products from recycled materials usually creates less water, land and air pollution than creating products using virgin materials.

Producing recycled white paper creates 74% less air pollution and 35% less water pollution than producing paper from virgin fibers.

Recycled food grease can be made into biodiesel fuel to decrease our need for gasoline.

Using recycled cans instead of extracting ore to make aluminum cans produces 95% less air pollution and 97% less water pollution.

#3. Recycling Reduces Worldwide Climate Changes.

Recycling helps with our climate problem by reducing the amount of greenhouse gasses being released into the atmosphere.

Recycling produces considerably less carbon than the creation of products from virgin material. This greatly helps to reduce the amount of unhealthy greenhouse gas omissions released into the atmosphere.

The largest source of human-caused methane comes from landfills. Methane is a greenhouse gas that is 21 times more dangerous than carbon dioxide. The less waste sent to landfills, the less greenhouse gasses will escape into our atmosphere.

#4. Recycling Saves Our Natural Resources And Protects Wildlife.

When we create new products by using recycled materials instead of virgin materials, we conserve the earth and forest, thus reducing the need to destroy wildlife habitats.

Recycling paper products saves millions of trees.

It also reduces the need to drill for oil or mine for precious minerals in pristine wilderness areas.

Using recycled materials uses less water, therefore helps to conserve our precious clean water.

It usually takes less energy when recycled items are the source material used to create a new product without starting from virgin materials.

Recycled items reduce the need for gathering virgin source materials, many of which can never be replenished.

#5. Recycling Is Good For The Economy.

The recycling process creates many more jobs than landfills ever will. For every one job at a landfill, there are ten jobs in recycling processing facilities and 25 jobs in recycling-based manufacturing.

Currently, the recycling industry employs more workers than the auto industry.

Purchasing products made from recycled materials creates a greater demand for more recycled goods, thus inspiring more companies to create more products from recycle material.

#6. Recycling Saves Money.

Recycling often turns out to be the least expensive waste management method for cities and towns that offer waste management services.

Although there may seem to be extra up-front costs of collecting and processing recyclables, these costs are usually offset by selling recyclable materials, which in turns makes recycling the cheaper option for the community.

By using recycled materials, companies can save on energy consumption, which keeps production costs down.

#7. Recycling Saves Energy.

Recycling usually takes less energy than creating a product from virgin materials.

It takes 95% less energy to create an aluminum can from recycled aluminum than using new aluminum from bauxite ore.

Recycling saves energy because the manufacturer doesn't have to produce something new from raw natural resources.

Percentage of energy saved by recycling compared with raw materials usage:
- Aluminum   95%
- Plastics   75%
- Steel   60%
- Glass   40%
- Newspaper   40%

Source "Environmental Benefits of Recycling" National Recycling coalition, 2005

By recycling about 30% of our waste every year, Americans could save the equivalent of 11.9 billion gallons of gasoline and reduce the greenhouse gases by an amount equivalent to taking 25 million cars off the road.

#8. Recycling Is Easy To Do!

Almost every city has at least one waste management service that handles some recyclable items or a location open to the public where recycled items can be taken.

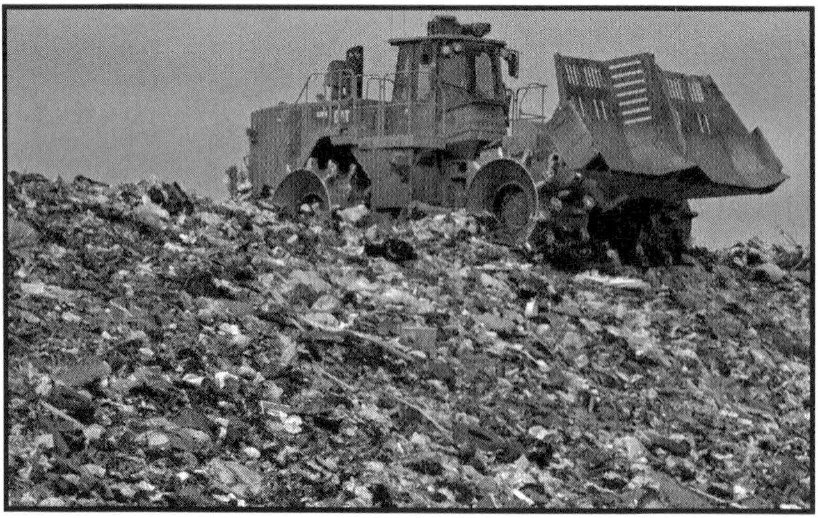

Chapter 6

Why Collect And Compost Food Waste?

As you read this chapter, I am sure that you will be amazed at how many items that normally ends up in a landfill could be composted instead.

Composting food and service ware waste yields significantly lower emissions of methane gas compared to the same amount of food waste decomposing in landfills.

Sending food waste into a garbage disposal unit and then into our wastewater treatment plants is not a good thing for the Earth. Garbage disposals use clean water to flush food waste down the drain. These food particles absorb water and that water then gets processed as solid waste, not liquid.

Be aware that these guidelines for what can be composted are relating to using a commercial composting facility.

Although many items can also be composted in a home compost pile, items like bioplastics need an extremely high level of heat to compost properly, so they would not be appropriate items to compost in your garden compost pile.

Also, meat items, even chicken bones, or dairy products like moldy cheese, can entice creatures such as raccoons, bears or dogs to root through a garden compost pile in search of easy food, so are not a good idea to compost around your home.

Bioplastics

Requiring food vendors to use biodegradable, compostable plastics, also known as bioplastics, can help reduce dependence on fossil fuels, inspire other manufacturers to develop more sustainable products, and divert a large amount of food waste from landfills.

Think about how all of these items could be turned into new rich soil to enrich the Earth, rather than becoming stinky, unusable waste sitting in a landfill releasing more methane gas into the atmosphere.

It is predicted that within the next 5 years, demand for bioplastics will increase by 35-40%.

As demand for bioplastics increases, so does the potential for mislabeling and false claims to be attached to products.

As more and more biodegradable products become available to purchase, it has already been seen that some manufacturers do not follow the proper guidelines for creating bioplastic that compost easily and properly. This has led to some confusion in the marketplace.

When choosing a supplier for bioplastics, be sure to research them thoroughly to be sure their products are properly labeled and follow industry standards for the rate it will take them to decompose.

Learn more about the potential problems and what to look for in a company when purchasing bioplastics at:

http://www.lanecounty.org/departments/pw/wmd/recycle/pages/eventrecyclingbinsanddurables.aspx

Composting Creates By-Products That Can Be Used To Improve Soil

When applied to land, compost has many Benefits.

- Improved soil fertility.
- Soil exhibits better water retention.
- Easier root penetration.
- Soil temperature stabilization.
- Topsoil is more stable.
- It helps to grow healthier, more nutritious plants.
- Reduces the need for chemical additives which decreases soil and ground water pollution.

Almost All Food Items Can Be Composted
Food Items That Can Be Composted:
- Produce trim from leafy vegetables and vegetable salads
- Day old breads and pastries, excess batter, spoiled bakery products
- Moldy breads, rolls and bagels
- Donuts, cookies and muffins
- Dairy products: cheese, yogurt, ice cream, misc. by-products
- Floral waste and trimmings from plants
- Leftovers that cannot be served again
- Plate scrapings - food waste
- Fruit and vegetable peelings and seeds
- Uneaten fruit and vegetable salads
- Spoiled fruits
- Frozen foods
- Freezer burned foods
- Coffee grounds/filters
- Tea bags
- Egg shells
- Noodles
- Onion skins
- Potatoes
- Rice
- Poultry
- Fish
- Meat*
- Bones*

*Meat trimmings (most facilities prohibit the inclusion of large bones or bulk quantities of grease, oils, and fats in the compost. Although these products are biodegradable, they are slow to decompose and may attract rodents or other animals. Local renderers are a better choice for handling significant quantities of this type of material.)

Compostable Food Service Products

Many food service items that are needed to serve food at Events are now available in compostable forms. Other items listed below have always been compostable.

Below is a list of items food vendors need to use that are biodegradable and can be composted.

Compostable food service and packaging items:
- Biodegradable service ware
- Bamboo based service ware, bowls and plates
- Compostable straws
- Corn based cups
- Paper plates and cups
- Paper napkins and towels
- PLA/corn base containers or tableware
- Paper trays
- Paper food wrappers
- Biodegradable gloves
- Any food contaminated paper products
- Wet or lightly waxed corrugated cardboard
- Cardboard egg cartons
- Corrugated boxes

As stated at the beginning of this chapter, I will bet you were surprised at some items that can be composted.

Items That Cannot Be Composted

Unfortunately there are also many materials used at most Events for food storage and preparation that cannot be composted or recycled.

Below is a list of items that must be sent to the landfill. Luckily these types of items make up only a small portion of the waste an Event will generate.

Items that cannot be composted:
- Foil wrappers
- Polystyrene foam
- Plastic gloves
- Plastic utensil (forks, spoons, knives, plates, cups, stir sticks, lids, etc.)
- Single serving containers (condiments, cream, etc.)
- Plastic and wire ties
- Plastic food wrap
- Plastic bags
- Plastic lids
- Shrink wrap or plastic film
- Plastic bottles (Many types of clean ones can be recycled.)
- Plastic buckets
- Plastic food containers
- Styrofoam
- Glass
- Metals

Exceptions
- Plastics that are biodegradable and made from corn or soy based materials can be composted.
- Plastic bags that are biodegradable and can be composted will be identified on the bags and can be verified at the following website:
www.bpiworld.org/BPI-Public/Approved/1.html

A huge challenge at outdoor Events is how busy the food vendors are during much of the Event. Most of them have very little staff and handling compostable waste is quite challenging for them.

They often will bag the compostable items in regular plastic bags. This means a *"Bin Monitor"* would have to slice open the bag and dump out the compostable items into the proper bin and dispose of the plastic bag in the trash. *This is a huge "Yuck" factor for "Bin Monitors".*

To avoid this challenge, consider having compostable plastic bags available for your food vendors to use to transport compostable items. Doing this could make a huge difference in how much compostable food waste is diverted from the Landfill.

The Best Way To Handle Liquid Waste

Events can make a difference by collecting liquid waste rather than having it tossed into the same container that landfill, recycled or compost waste is collected.

It is best if liquids can be collected in a separate bucket and sent back to a wastewater facility.

Some portalet companies allow liquid waste to be dumped into the units for removal at the end of the day. Just be sure no greasy residue is dumped into the units!

Using a chicken wire screen over a gallon plastic bucket makes it easy to keep out lemons or other items that are not liquid. Having lemons or other food items in the liquid that is dumped into the portalets causes problems when the portalets are emptied. To keep your supplier happy, take this extra step to avoid blockages and disgruntled portalet employees.

The buckets and chicken wire screens can be cleaned up at the end of the Event and reused for many years.

Chapter 7

Case Study-Prime Example Of How To Create A Sustainable Festival

Commonwheel Artists Co-op Annual Labor Day Art Festival (Art Festival) has proven that it is possible to create a more sustainable outdoor festival starting from scratch in its first attempt.

Everyone who pitched in to make it possible found that doing so was very rewarding on many levels. Many of the original volunteers have returned each year to help the Art Festival reach an even higher waste diversion goal.

This book was written to help others get a "jump-start" on how to plan a sustainable Event and help organizers avoid some of the "learning curve" challenges that the Commonwheel Art Festival had the first few years it worked towards becoming a more sustainable Art Festival.

Commonwheel Artists Annual Labor Day Art Festival As A Case Study

I, Julia L. Wright, have coordinated the Commonwheel Artists Annual Labor Day Art Festival for 34 of its 40 years, starting in 1976 as the assistant coordinator and having taken a few "sabbaticals" over the years.

In the spring of 2009 I went to a conference for Colorado Festival organizers. At this conference, I attended a seminar where presenters talked about holding "Zero-Waste" Events. Their presentation got me really motivated to consider the possibility of making the Commonwheel's Art Festival more sustainable in some way.

I brought the idea back to the Art Festival committee and they also got excited, but with reservations about the cost to hire that company. Commonwheel's Art Festival has a very limited budget. We realized their fee made it impossible to afford hiring the speaker's company to put all the pieces in place to be a totally Zero-Waste festival.

It was quickly decided that we did want to create a more sustainable event and we discussed some of steps we could consider taking to make our Art Festival more sustainable.

The Commonwheel Artists Co-op, which basically is a Gallery for its members, barely has enough members to fulfill all the jobs it takes to have the Art Festival run smoothly each year. And we doubted that many members would want to take on more jobs, even if they were totally onboard with the vision of a sustainable Art Festival. We also were fairly certain that the number of volunteers it would take to make this work could not be found within our membership. So we knew we would have to go outside our Co-op membership to achieve this goal.

Over the next few days, I sent out a few emails to friends and environmentally focused groups in the area explaining the Art Festival's committee's wish to create a more sustainable Art Festival that year. In that email, I had proposed just adding recycling stations and wanted their feedback.

We got extremely lucky and found some people who also got really energized by this idea for our whole community. They suggested a meeting where they offered to help make it happen.

All of the people who responded favorably wanted to include composting as an element for creating a more sustainable festival. They all knew that compostables actually created the biggest amount of landfill waste at most Events.

One woman was the Chair of the Manitou Springs Climate Protection Campaign. She had already begun a campaign to convince the City Council and citizens of Manitou Springs that for the sake or our roads and the environment that it was time to have just one Waste Collection provider for our small hilly town. She knew that this provider would have to be able to offer Single Stream Recycling along with its Waste Collection for the most reasonable cost to its citizens.

Another woman had a recycling company for electronics and wanted to get the word out about how important that was for maintaining a healthier planet in the future.

Next, we had our first planning meeting to define what we would need to do to make the Art Festival more sustainable that very year.

One challenge was that all the Art Festival applications had been printed without the information stating what we would expect from food vendors and artists. This meant we had to do a lot of extra phone calls that year after we held the jury session to determine which food vendors would be participating that year. We needed to let them know about the extra requirements they would comply with to participate as a food vendor that year.

Right after the jury session, we sent out emails to all the food vendors and artists who were accepted into the Art Festival. In these emails we explained our sustainable goals for the Art Festival.

The Festival sent out a letter offering a total refund to any food vendor who did not want to comply with the new guidelines. None of the accepted food vendors chose to opt out of the Art Festival.

The sustainable committee created a guideline for what food service items had to be recyclable and what food service items had to be compostable.

In all of our communications it was clearly stated that all Styrofoam serving items would be banned from this event.

One committee member did some research and found suppliers for the proper type of service ware to be used that would be compostable or recyclable and sent that information to all of the food vendors. When searching for eco-friendly product suppliers, we looked for the best prices and as locally available as possible.

A month before the Art Festival, one of the sustainable committee members called all 12 of the food vendors. She had a one-on-one conversation with each one in order to be sure they clearly understood what was expected of them and that they were bringing the proper items to serve their food items at the Art Festival.

During the second year of working towards becoming a Waste Wise Art Festival, members of Transition Town Manitou

52 *Case Study-Prime Example Of How To Create A Sustainable Festival*

Springs came to some of the planning meetings. They helped gather volunteers and run the booth at the Art Festival where eco-friendly organizations could share their information.

In the following years, leaders of Transition Town Manitou Springs now head up this project.

In 2014, the Art Festival is going into its 6th year as a sustainable Art Festival.

Each year we have improved the diversion rate and gotten many more members of the community involved. We learned numerous lessons each year that I have shared in this book.

Most of what we have learned these past five years will work for every type of Event – large or small.

A few of the ideas you will read about in this book are on our "wish list" for becoming an even more sustainable Art Festival. Others are ones we have successfully incorporated into the Commonwheel Artists Labor Day Art Festival.

Some of these pieces written about here are a bit more difficult to incorporate into our small, well-established outdoor Art Festival. Yet in other areas and at different types of Events, they might be the perfect fit for your Event to begin incorporating to create a more sustainable Event.

Chapter 8

What Level Of Sustainability Is The Goal For Your Event?

It is always important to define goals for any project you engage in to refer to for gauging your success upon completion.

Goal setting is extremely critical when creating a sustainable Event. And the Event organizer must be sure everyone involved understands these goals and how they can help reach them.

Setting Goals

You will want to set solid goals that relate to each of the steps you want to implement the first year and include an outline of your plans for future years.

These goals should revolve around what types of sustainable steps you will take the first year and in future years.

You can take a small step the first year. Then, once the first steps prove easy to do and you have motivated other members of your organization and community by the results, add pieces in the following years.

You will want to have a goal for how much energy can be saved and/or how much waste can be diverted from the landfill. Add to your goals and plan any other sustainable ideas you have read about in this book that you would like to implement to positively effect the environment at your Waste Wise Event.

Action Plan

Once your goals are set, take time to discuss the various types of actions it will take to achieve the goals and outcome you have defined for your sustainable Event.

Be sure to take into consideration how many volunteers you will need to implement these actions.

Next, your organization will need to decide if it can handle all the details by itself.

You might want to consider appointing or hiring one person whose responsibility will be to oversee that all planning choices are made with environmental sustainability in mind.

Or, you may want to seek out another organization, such as Transition Town, that will want to take it on as a project that fits in with their mission statement.

Share Your Goals And Plan

Once you have your vision plan and your goals written up, you will need to discuss this plan with all the types of organizations and vendors that it will impact that will be part of your Event.

You may have to seek out some creative solutions to reach your goals.

Don't hesitate to share your plan with your larger community base using Facebook, Twitter, emails or newspaper articles to get the help you need.

Members of the Event staff, volunteers and vendors need to be made fully aware of what they will need to do to comply with the sustainable choices necessary to reach the goals of your plan.

You will also want to ensure that your sponsors are onboard with your goals and can adhere to the Event's sustainable strategies. Sharing your plan with them as soon as it is in a written form is one way to assist them in being able to understand what you are asking of them.

You need to have a clear plan of action for members of the staff that will be hiring service providers, doing the advertising and training volunteers at the event. Determine who will be able to train other members of the team on procedures that will be used to implement the plan.

Let everyone involved know how to contact the point person in your organization who will be available to answer any questions or address any concerns the service providers may have regarding what is expected of them.

How Will You Measure Your Success?

Another point to discuss is the various ways and means you will use to track and measure the successes you anticipate.

Keep it as simple as possible.

One option is to create a chart that counts the number of trash bags, pounds of paper collected and bins filled with recyclables and/or compostable items versus landfill bins, etc.

Create spreadsheets to track various aspects of your sustainable plan to show what worked and what will need improvement in the coming years.

You will want to establish a baseline for resources used at past Events and set some goals for reducing those numbers.

Or, start with this Event and keep a record to compare your successes achieved at this first Event and watch to see how those numbers improve at future Events.

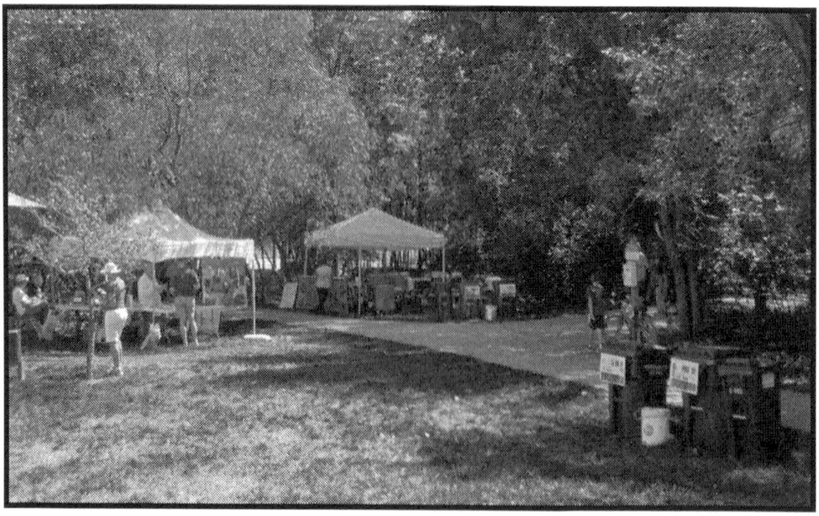

Chapter 9

What All The Vendors Need To Know

To have a truly successful sustainable Event you need to disseminate information to all your participants, not just food vendors, before, during and after the event.

Everyone at the Event needs to be involved to make it work as smoothly and easily as possible to reach your sustainable goals.

Getting Started

Before an Event starts, you will want to educate all types of participants that will be at your Event about your Event's sustainable goals.

Start by sending an email to all participants explaining what measures will be implemented by your organization to make the Event as sustainable as possible.

Clearly define the Event's sustainable goals.

Describe what they can expect to see happening at the Event to achieve your sustainable goals.

Include tips on how to reduce materials they might be thinking of using. Suggest ideas for reusable or compostable items they might want to consider using for their displays or packaging of items they bring and/or will sell at the Event.

Share alternative transportation suggestions and where to find that information relating to their locations.

Suggest ways participants can take part at your Event and beyond to participate in the Event's sustainable theme.

During The Event

Throughout the day, announce reminders to participants abut the sustainable measures being implemented at the Event.

Be sure that bins for recyclable or compostable items are well marked with easy to understand signage and located next to trash bins. Graphic images of what goes in each type of bin works best.

Have volunteers check on the bins to be sure the proper items are being disposed of in their designated bins. They need to have "trash grabbers" and wear rubber gloves to they can easily sort out items placed in the wrong bins by the visitors.

You might consider having an erasable board at the exit points where attendees could mark an *"X"* under *"yes"* or *"no"*, in answer to a few simple questions regarding their experience of your sustainable efforts.

Ways To Engage All Of Your Vendors, Not Just Food Vendors

The types of packaging used at an event will determine what types of waste are produced. By considering the best alternatives for all types of packaging, as well as reducing the amount of packaging used, the amount of waste generated and disposed of at landfills can be greatly reduced.

It is important that all vendors understand that Styrofoam packaging is not acceptable.

Offering reusable bags with the Events logo on it for sale or for free can be helpful in cutting down the amount of bags used at the Event. This is a great advertising tool that will get your logo seen farther out in the community when it is used by the attendee when shopping elsewhere.

There are many paper products available that contain recycled content. Encourage your vendors to seek these out when purchasing paper bags. Larger items can be carried into and away from an event in cardboard boxes or other types of recyclable or reusable containers. Fragile or breakable objects can be wrapped in newspaper rather than using Styrofoam peanuts or bubble wrap.

For a truly Waste Wise Event, using plastic bags for any reason should be avoided.

Announce Your Success

After the Event ends, you need to take some time to gather data regarding how much waste was routed away from the landfill.

Announce your success in an email to your participants.

Shout your success to the world by releasing a Press Release thanking those who attended and share your sustainable Event's success story.

Tweet about it and write about it on Facebook.

If you have a great picture showing the different amounts of waste that was sent to be recycled versus heading to the landfill – use it!

(See Chapter 14 for the more details on how to do this.)

Event In Review

After the Event send out an email survey to your participants. Ask them to answer a few questions relating to their experience of your sustainable Event.

Survey Monkey.com is one of the easiest and free ways to do this. It keeps the respondents anonymous. This often means more people will be willing to answer your questions and add comments.

Consider asking them to share with you any problems they encountered complying with the requirements, any public feedback they heard and what they liked about it. Make it short and simple, but let them know it is important for you to have their feedback to improve the following year's Event.

(See Chapter 15 for the best ways to gather this information.)

STRAWBERRY Lemonade
STRAWBERRY Lemonade
CINNAMON ROASTED ALMONDS
CINNAMON ROASTED ALMONDS
STRAWBERRY LEMONADE

Chapter 10

Food Vendors Are Key Players At A Sustainable Event

Having the full participation of your food vendors can really make a huge difference in how much waste gets into the proper containers to be diverted from the landfill.

Communicating your goals and requirements for what you expect of your food vendors needs to be very clear and repeated more than once in emails and phone conversations.

If this is the first year for your sustainable Event or when inviting new food vendors to participate for the first time, someone in your organization needs to have a personal conversation with each of those food vendors a couple of months before Event.

Emails are great for follow-ups and to remind past food vendors about the requirements. But it is best to start the conversation about your sustainable goals by making a phone call to your food vendors. A phone call will prove to be very helpful to avoid problems at the Event caused by a food vendor not understanding or claiming they missed seeing the emails. This is especially true if this is the first year you are adding sustainable requirements to a well-established Event or bringing in a food vendor who has not participated in the Event before.

Whether your Event is to be held indoors or outside, if you have food vendors that are not caterers, but individual participants, you need to give them some guidelines that are very clear and easy to follow.

If your Event is to be catered or you will be working with an on-site food provider, you will need to discuss options with them that will be acceptable for your sustainable Event.

Create Clear Guidelines

There must be very clear and explicitly detailed guidelines for food vendors explaining what they can and cannot use to serve various types of food and beverage items they will be bringing to the Event.

This cannot be said too many times. It is extremely important all food vendors understand absolutely NO Styrofoam will be allowed for any service items at the Event.

You also don't want to allow a mix of plastic style cups for cold drinks. A standardized requirement needs to be set up, and communicated, to all food and beverage vendors. Clearly explain that all cold drink cups must be of the style you have determined will work best for your event. If your event is only doing recycling, then you will want to require cold drinks to be served in recyclable cups.

If you have composting available, you might want to consider requiring all cold beverage cups to be biodegradable, though keep in mind those are a bit more expensive for the vendor to purchase. Commonwheel found requiring that all beverage cups be compostable was the simplest way to avoid any confusion about which bin a person should to toss a beverage item into.

Most biodegradable beverage cups have a printed message stating what they are made of, but for *"Bin Monitors"* it can be a nightmare trying to sort out the plastic recyclables from the biodegradable ones that confused patrons placed in the wrong bins.

All hot drinks must be served in compostable paper cups – no Styrofoam coffee cups allowed! Even if you don't have composting bins available, the energy it takes to make a compostable cup is much less than any other type of hot beverage cup.

Requiring the use of biodegradable serving items saves energy and precious resources even if they end up in a landfill.

Flatware (spoons, forks, knives) must be made from biodegradable materials. The reasoning behind this is, even if you don't offer composting and they are sent to the landfill, they took less energy to create. Biodegradable service ware is made from renewable resources including sugar cane, potato or cornstarch and contains no toxic chemicals.

Wooden chopsticks can be suggested as an option for food vendors offering Oriental foods.

There are many types of biodegradable plates and clamshells on the market.

Simple, thin or heavy paper plates can be composted with food on them. Many are available that have been made with recycled materials and you can request your food vendors look for these type of plates.

Straws are impossible to recycle. They are either trash or compost and are usually unnecessary. Although there are now more compostable straws available than when we started, they are one of the items people have the most trouble figuring out where to dispose of properly.

Eco-Friendly Serving Products

Do some research and find sources for eco-friendly service products that might be available in your area, or some that have the best prices when purchased in large quantities.

Send out an email in which you share these source suggestions for eco-friendly serving products so each food vendor doesn't have to do this same time-consuming type of research. They will grumble less about the requirements if you supply them with the best sources possible.

It might be a good idea to have some items for sale at the Event in case someone brings the wrong type of service item. This is not always possible, or affordable, for small groups.

Keep in mind, it would be very difficult for a food vendor to go out and buy the proper item if they have brought the wrong type of food service items to an Event. Hopefully, all your pre-event communications were clear enough that no food vendor makes this type of mistake. But be aware, it can happen.

Here are a couple of distributors for food service supplies to begin your research.

http://www.ecoproducts.com/ *(Located in Boulder, CO.)*
http://www.ultragreenhome.com/

(More resources for buying eco-friendly products can be found in Chapter 17 at the end of this book.)

Food Packaging Ideas

To achieve the goal of having the least amount of packaging items ending up as waste items at an Event, the most important step is to avoid unnecessary packaging in the first place.

When disposal of packaging is unavoidable, encourage your food vendors to use biodegradable (compostable) paper, including wax paper products made from recycled content. They take less energy to produce and are easy to compost if that option is available.

Ask your food vendors to consider whether each type of packaging they are considering using is necessary, and if it is not, suggest they don't purchase or use it.

Look at their menus and share any helpful suggestions you have to eliminate the need for packaging or service ware.

Suggest to food vendors that ice cream cones are edible and eliminate the need for other types of containers. Paper wraps for burritos or crepes work as well as a plate. Waxed paper wrappers work well for sandwiches, burgers and turkey legs.

Whenever possible, suggest ways they can avoid the use of non-recyclable, plastic and (banned) polystyrene products and packaging for the bulk items they are bringing to the Event.

Food Service Concerns For Indoor Or Catered Events

Have someone on your organizational team meet in person, or by phone, to discuss your sustainable goals with the caterer, Executive Chef, or facilities manager that will be providing food for the attendees, presenters and/or entertainers.

Have them check into the possibility of creating a menu using natural or organic seasonal foods and beverages. You will want to have some ideas to suggest to them about what is available locally relating to the season that your Event will be held. Ask them if they can use locally grown foods in their meal plans. If they are serving seafood dishes, make sure they come from a sustainable seafood source. If there greenhouses or aquaponics businesses that can provide organic produce or fish in the area that you know about, share that contact information with them.

Since there are many attendees that have special dietary requirements ask if the food service provider or caterer if they can provide a vegetarian or vegan meal option. Ask if they would consider creating at least one totally meatless meal as a step towards having more sustainable food offerings at your Event.

Another food concern relates to having a gluten-free option included in the menu offerings. Ask the food service provider or caterer if they can provide a pleasing, totally gluten-free meal if this is one of the attendees dietary requests.

You will want to request that they use large containers for sweeteners, beverages, condiments and other food items instead of individual serving packets, cans or bottles.

Serving coffee, ice tea and water in glasses or mugs that will be washed and reused would be an important factor to consider when choosing a caterer or venue. You don't want to have tons of plastic bottles used at a sit down meal when glasses will serve just as well for serving beverages.

You want to have them closely estimate food amounts that will be needed by giving them an accurate as possible head count to minimize waste.

Ask them how they handle leftover edible food items. Find out if they have a way to distribute those types of items to a nearby food kitchen. If not, suggest they check into this concept.

If your event is offering composting services, be sure they have a proper system set-up in the kitchen. Have a conversation with the caterer, chef and food service team to be assured they all understand how important it is to gather all food preparation scraps for composting. When using an on-site food service, you will want to supply them with easy to access compost bins in the kitchen area.

Place compost bins next to the food service area, matched with all other well labeled trash bins for participants to deposit leftover food items in at the end of each meal.

Find out from the manager of the venue if they use reusable tablecloths, napkins, plates, flatware, and beverage containers. This should have been discovered when looking at and choosing a venue. But, if you are making the switch to creating a more sustainable Event and have been in the same venue in the previous year, it is now time to have this discussion.

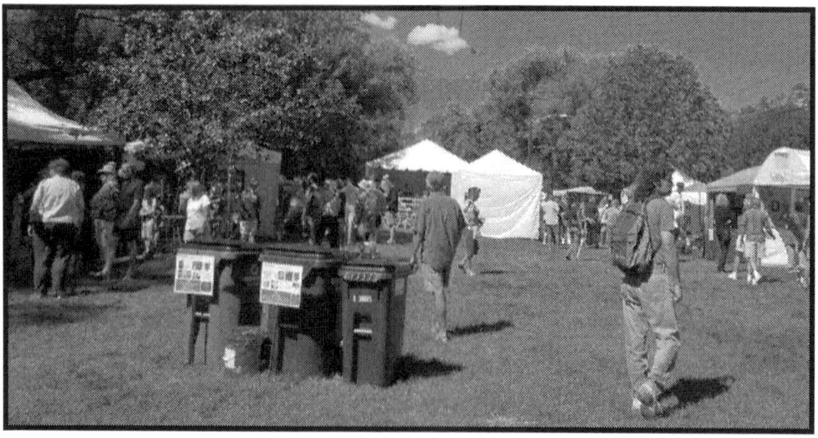

Chapter 11

Waste Collection And Disposal

All waste, landfill trash, recyclable items and compost collected at the Event must be transported to a licensed waste recycling and/or disposal facility.

For most outdoor Events, it will be up to your organization to make arrangements with a Waste Service Provider to collect and dispose of waste created at the Event.

Most indoor venues have contracts in place to handle waste items. You will need to have a conversation with the venue's manager to discern if they can incorporate recycling or composting into their waste handling.

If recycling is not available there, you might want to search for another venue.

But remember, if you must use a venue that doesn't recycle anything, you can still implement the simplest recycling idea of just collecting paper items and recycle them yourself. Clean paper items that might get tossed out after the Event are easy to gather in boxes or reusable containers at the exits and different rooms at any venue.

Waste Collection Stations

At your Event's site, you will need to provide the proper type of collection receptacles for each type of waste you are gathering.

Signage is very important to make it easy for the public to discern where to dispose of each type of waste they are holding in their hands.

You will always want to have all types of waste collection bins near a landfill waste container to avoid contamination.

Before your Event, take some time and think about the best ways to create Waste Collection Stations for your Event.

Create a map of the site that includes where to locate the Waste Collection Stations. Taking the time in advance of the Event to discern where the most advantageous places around an outdoor or indoor venue to place your Waste Stations will save much time and energy during and after the Event.

Separate groups of Waste Collection Stations should be provided for the public and food vendors. Every Waste Collection Stations needs to be comprised of one bin for each type of waste you are collecting and clustered together. They may even require a bit of different signage depending on where they will be placed and who will be accessing them for disposing of waste at the Event.

Separate containers for each type of waste collected need to be provided at every Waste Station.

There are four possible types of waste collection receptacles that you might need to offer. The number and types of waste collection receptacles will depend upon the type of waste management services you are using for waste disposal at your Event.

Having signs with pictures, or at the very least a list of the items that can be tossed into each type of bin will help the general public understand where to dispose of each type of waste item they have in their hands.

Attendees at all types of Events are usually in some state of overwhelm just trying to absorb all the information, entertainment or visuals that they came to see. Many won't take the time to think about what to do with waste items without really good signage.

That said, it is very important that each type of receptacle is clearly labeled. Signs need to clearly designate which bin is to be used for landfill trash, single stream recyclables, liquids and biodegradable compost items. Graphic images are the easiest way for an attendee to determine what type of waste goes into which bin.

You might think you don't need to label the one for collecting liquids, but it would be better to label it than to find gallons of liquids in your other waste bins. You can even add "No Liquids" as part of the signage for all other types of waste bins to assure people don't just dump cups full of liquids into them.

At indoor Events, having overhead signage on waste and recycling stations assists Event participants in locating stations.

At outdoor Events, it is especially important to have signs with pictures of some of the items that confuse people the most posted in front of the bins. Pictures, along with written words, are very helpful and make the job of the *"Bin Monitors"* much easier. Make sure there is a written list of what type of items you know will be used by food vendors at your Event clearly visible in front of the waste receptacle they should be disposed in to help everyone dispose of their waste items in the proper bin.

Where To Locate Waste Collection Stations

Waste Collection Stations need to be located where they are most required and easy to access.

Public Waste Stations need to be located in walkways, exits and eating areas.

How many bins that need to be available at each Waste Collection Station will depend upon the types of waste management services are being used at your event. There may be just two types of bins: landfill waste and recycling. Or, there may need to be bins for co-mingled recycling, landfill waste, liquid waste and biodegradable compost items. Or, some other combination of bins needed depending on what type of waste will be diverted from the landfill at your Event.

Waste Collection Stations for food vendors at outdoor Events are a bit trickier to locate properly. Take a look at the layout in the Food Court area and decide how many Waste Collection Stations will be needed to service your food vendors as efficiently as possible.

You will want to be certain the food and beverage vendors have an adequate number of containers. Keeping that in mind, you will want to make it as easy as possible for them to comply, without having to set up an excessive number of Waste Collection Stations inside of individual booths.

If space is an issue, you may need to assign a staff person to assist the food vendors in disposing of their waste into the proper containers throughout the Event.

Or, food vendors may need assistance from Event volunteers to get their waste bins emptied during a particularly busy time during the Event. Consider having a volunteer check with the food vendors a couple of times a day to help them comply with the requirements properly.

Check And Recheck Again

It is extremely important that volunteers check on the landfill waste containers, single stream recycling and biodegradable compost item bins at regularly scheduled intervals during the Event to help avoid contamination. It is so much easier to pick out the items that have been disposed of in the wrong bins when they can be easily seen on the surface instead of deeply buried under other items.

The volunteers who will be emptying the bins need to be sure that the contents get taken to the proper destination collection bins before they become so full that items begin to spill out of the bins and litter the nearby area or get carried off by the wind.

You want to make every effort to avoid contamination of the large waste collection receptacles or roll-offs. These bins will hold the various types of waste gathered from smaller bins until it is transported to its proper waste handling facility.

Be sure to clearly label the large waste receptacles with signs saying: *"Trash Only"*, *"Recycle Only"* or *"Compost Only"*. It would be a real shame if some uninformed person, or tired vendor, dumps the wrong type of waste into a large bin and contaminates a Recycle Bin with trash or compost, thus wasting all the hard work done by the *"Bin Monitors"* during the Event.

Collection Bins

Bins for the Waste Collection Stations can be standard 32-gallon roll-offs provided by your local waste contractors or other containers your organization finds suitable.

At the Commonwheel Art Festival, we tried a few different ideas the first couple of years, but the standard roll-offs worked the best for many reasons.

One advantage of using roll-offs is that you can have an extra roll-off unit beyond the number of waste stations at the Event. This makes it easy to just keep switching them out, leaving the empty one in place when a full one is rolled to the main collection area for emptying. This way no Waste Collection Station is ever without its full contingent of all types of bins for the various types of waste to be collected.

Pulling a roll-off unit is so much easier on volunteers than having to carry bags of trash through a crowded Event. And, the *"ick"* factor of carrying slightly odorous or dripping compost bags through a crowd is really something you want to avoid if at all possible to make this job less difficult for everyone involved.

Our Waste Service Management provider, Bestway Disposal, uses different colored bins for the different types of waste materials that are collected. This makes it easy to discern what goes where for our volunteer *"Bin Guardians"* and *"Waste Rustlers"*.

Since Commonwheel's waste service provider had to wash all of the bins when they got returned before they could be used again, they didn't care if the compost bins or recycling bins had bags lining the bins to capture the waste. This allowed our volunteers to just wheel them to the proper large collection receptacle and pour the contents from the roll-offs into the larger waste receptacle without having to worry about removing a plastic bag from the recycled items. It also eliminated having to buy expensive biodegradable bags for the compost bins.

But if your waste management company doesn't like the idea of your not using bags in the roll-offs, you need to take a few extra steps. Or if you can't get roll-offs supplied, you need to have the proper types of bags to collect the various types of waste that will be diverted from the landfill.

Recyclable materials can be collected using large plastic bags, but when the recyclables are dumped into the end collection bin, the bags must be removed, or the load will be considered contaminated. If your volunteers are careful when handling them, these bags can be used many times.

There are biodegradable plastic bags that can be used in the bins for collecting compost. They really are worth the extra expense to make it easier for food vendors and volunteers.

Emptying a plastic bag filled with biodegradable material can be rather messy. At an outdoor Event, there is rarely an easy or convenient cleanup station if a volunteer gets their hands covered with gooey stuff.

If you have an outdoor Event that lasts longer than three days in the summer, the compost collection bins could become a bit rank, but we haven't had any problem like that yet.

Bears have been another challenge at our outdoor art festival. Our night security has had to scare them away from the large collection bins. They usually easily leave the area if a bright light shines on them accompanied with loud noises. Having bins that are sturdy and can be locked also is a deterrent to bears or other wildlife like raccoons and skunks.

Liquid Waste

Liquid waste can be collected in a standard 5-gallon plastic bucket and that can often be emptied into the portable restrooms provided for the Event.

You will want to secure a chicken wire screen on top of the liquid bin containers. This is necessary to prevent solid food products, such as lemon slices from a fresh lemonade vendor, from being dumped into the portable restrooms or wherever you dump the collected liquids.

It is up to the Event organizer to get approval from the portable restroom provider if you want to dump excess liquid waste into their tanks.

Most portable restroom companies will be OK with the liquid waste being dumped into them if they do not have other foreign objects in them, so the screening is an important factor for keeping them happy and not clogging the "honey" collection hoses.

If you have access to indoor plumbing, again, screening out anything that is not liquid is very important to not clog up the system.

Most items that get screened are compostable, so that is a big plus for getting more waste into the proper container and kept out of the landfill.

Grease

It is the responsibility of your food vendors at both outdoor and indoor Events to take the grease they use for cooking away from the Event. They must be held responsible to dispose of grease properly on their own.

You might want to do some research to see if there is any business in your area that creates Biodiesel fuel from used cooking grease. If you find one, contact them and ask them if they want to come to the Event and collect all the grease that may be generated by your food vendors. Offer them a free booth or a place to put their business cards and brochures at your Information Booth or registration table.

At the very least, give them mention in your Event's advertising flyers and/or on your Facebook page to encourage them to do this service.

Human Waste

Portable restroom companies that collect human waste have become more and more eco-minded in our region. The products they purchase and use are much more environmentally friendly than in the past.

There are questions you can ask to determine if the company is a "green" company and a fit for your Event.

Ask if the toilet paper used in the units meets EPA certified procurement guidelines. To do that, it would have a minimum of 95% recycled content of which 20% is post consumer and has 95% less packaging waste than standard roll toilet paper. Are both the core and packaging recycled and recyclable?

Do the paper towels they will be using meet EPA certified procurement guidelines. Do they have a minimum of 95% recycled content of which 50% is post consumer?

Are all of the cleaning products to be used biodegradable, formaldehyde free, contain no petrochemicals and have not been tested on animals?

Is the anti-bacterial hand gel sanitizer biodegradable? the hand gel should not contain parabens and be formaldehyde free. Are they made from renewable resources? Is the packaging (bag and box) recyclable?

One would assume that most of the products used are purchased in bulk, which reduces the amount of packaging that will be recycled or end up in a landfill. Still you might ask them about their purchasing habits as a way to check in on how they look at sustainability.

You will also want to ask some questions regarding what type of solution is used in the waste tanks that breaks down the waste and controls odor.

- Is the tank solution formaldehyde free?
- Is the tank solution 100% biodegradable?
- Does it contain petrochemicals?
- Was it tested on animals?
- Will it not harm the environment in any way?
- Are all components used in the product safe to breath or come in contact with a person's skin?

If the salesperson you talk with does not know these answers, ask them to find out for you or let you speak with someone that does have the answers.

Be sure they understand how it is important for them to answer these questions correctly for you to be confident they will be a fit for your Sustainable Event.

End Of Day Vigilance

To ensure a successful Waste Wise Event, you will need to have one staff person or volunteer assigned to remain after the Event is closed to the public each night to facilitate the proper disposal of waste by the exhibitors.

Exhibitors and food vendors take at least an hour after closing to shut down their booths. They need to be able to have access to the proper waste receptacles. At the end of a long day, the vendors are usually very tired and in a hurry to get away from the venue. So it is very important to have a *"Bin Monitor"* stationed at the large collection receptacles after the end of the Event to avoid having those bins contaminated by the wrong type of waste landing in them. Or sometimes a tired vendor will just want to throw everything in the landfill collection bin, but that will skew your numbers for how much could have gone elsewhere.

Make sure if the large containers are locked up that at least one of the smaller roll away bins are easily visible, clearly labeled and accessible to any vendors who needs to dispose of waste items after the Event has closed.

A Short Cautionary Tale

Commonwheel's Art Festival ran into problems around the end of day disposal by food vendors when someone locked all of the compost and trash containers.

The smaller roller collection bins were all stacked and jumbled together in a small area making them difficult to access or use. That meant the only place vendors could toss their trash was into the large recycling bin. And a couple did just that.

One of the volunteers actually climbed into that large bin and cleaned it out. Not a recommended practice, but that person was determined to not have the whole recycling bin discounted for a small amount of trash being intermingled with recyclables.

Items That Must Go To The Landfill

There is some trash that just can't be recycled or composted.
No matter how hard you try to avoid having actual trash at your Event, some of these types of items will show up.

Foil wrappers with food on them and plastic food wrap cannot be recycled.

Regular plastic gloves used by most food vendors to handle food must be considered trash also.

If you are not doing composting and requiring food vendors to use compostable utensils, none of the plastic utensil (forks, spoons, knives, plates, cups, stir sticks, lids, etc.) can be recycled. Plastic straws cannot be recycled either. The food on them and the type of plastic used to make them means they must go to a landfill.

Single serving containers (condiments, cream, etc.) will be landfill bound.

Plastic bags, shrink wrap or thin plastic film used to cover foods and the plastic or wire ties that are used to close bags can't be recycled or composted.

Any type of heavy plastic containers including buckets and plastic bottles must go into the trash.

Any metal item, other than aluminum cans, and some steel cans that don't have food residue, will end up in the landfill also.

Styrofoam and polystyrene foam containers need to be banned from your Event to avoid having them there. But if some show up, they are headed to landfill.

Some recycling companies do accept glass. Be sure to ask first before tossing them into recycling bins.

Chapter 12

Volunteers Needed

Most organizations that want to create a Waste Wise Event will need to enlist the help of many volunteers to make it as successful as possible.

You might be able to find a sponsor in your area that wants to have some positive eco-friendly advertising for their company and would be willing to inject some cash into sponsoring the Event. Such a sponsor would allow you to hire people to help at the Event. Unfortunately, these types of sponsors are not always easy to find.

On the other hand, there are many organizations and businesses that have a strong belief that creating a more sustainable world is the right thing to do and are willing to put their time and energy into making it happen.

Where To Find Volunteers

There are many places you can reach out to find volunteers. These are some suggestions for places to start:
- Transition Town Chapters
- Community Colleges
- 4-year Colleges and Universities
- Girl and Boy Scout Troops
- Groups focused on the Environment
- Friend and family Members
- People working within your organization
- Groups that need to do Community Service
- Sierra Club Chapters
- Garden Clubs
- Hiking Clubs

If you have a local Transition Town chapter in your area, seek it out and ask for help from their members.

Transition Town chapters are comprised of many types of businesses and individuals focused on ways to be create sustainable focused businesses and lifestyles. This makes them the perfect group to approach, as they are invested in creating a more sustainable world on many levels and are looking for ways to share their knowledge with the general public.

Some chapters may already have many projects they work on, but they usually have a huge network that includes other groups or businesses that are willing to provide volunteers to help at your event.

Or, they may know of the perfect person to help guide your organization through some of the more challenging parts or creating a sustainable Event.

If there is no Transition Town chapter near your Event's location, seek out a PermaCulture teacher in your region. This teacher could possibly put you in touch with some of their past, and/or current students that may be willing to take this on as a big project.

Boy Scout and Girl Scout troops need to do all types of community service projects to earn merit badges. You can offer them a location that they can set up a booth to tell other young people about their troop and the benefits of joining the Scouts in exchange for their volunteering at your Event.

The one challenge with using these types of groups is they are usually young and not able to handle the lifting and emptying of heavy roll-offs. So you would need to enlist the help of the Scout Masters or find other volunteers who would just handle that part.

Some colleges have an eco-program that offers a credit or requires their students to participate in a sustainable Event in their area. If your Event is held in the summer, it is a bit more difficult to connect with that type of volunteer, unless there is a very large group of students attending classes during the summer.

If you foresee continuing your Event for many years, you might want to approach your local 2-year or 4-year local College or University with a plan that proposes ways for students that volunteered at your Event to earn a credit for various reasons in one of the standard programs.

The plan could show how they would learn about how important it is to do community service and/or how waste management is changing. It also fits into agricultural curriculums when composting is part of the Waste Wise Event.

Each student would be required to write a report on what they learn, or how the event could run more smoothly with changes they would suggest.

Part of the plan could be for them to devise and implement ways to measure the amount of waste diverted from the landfill and any other energy saving pieces that were part of your Event.

Every area has various types of groups that need to do public service for different reasons. There are various *"Kids At Risk"* types of organizations that involve the kids doing community service as an important part of their program as a way to "give back" to their community. This type of service allows kids to learn more about how to be good stewards of the Earth and receive praise for doing something that is positive. It is amazing how many kids in this type of program have never heard the words *"Thank you"* for anything they had ever done in the past.

Positive reinforcement brings about change.

At the Commonwheel Art Festival, we have worked with a "Kids at Risk" school program for about 10 years. We have seen how it changes their perception of themselves when shown appreciation for something they do with a positive impact. When some of these kids see and interact with artists who earn a living selling artwork or having a food booth, it gives them ideas that there could be a place in the world for someone that corrals their talents onto a more acceptable path. This interaction helps them to think about what talents they have that could be marketable and sets them upon a path of looking at their future life choices in a new and more positive way.

An Event organizer can approach the management of such a group and put a proposal together for them to consider. This probably works best for outdoor events, but any Event coordinator could try it.

Scheduling And Contact Information For Volunteers

At any Event that uses volunteers, it is necessary to create a volunteer schedule.

It is especially important to have a clear schedule for volunteers working the waste management side of a Waste-Free Event.

In most cases, volunteers are willing to work for a three or four hour shift in a day, but not much longer.

Look at the jobs that need to be done and determine how many volunteers it will take to fill them based on three or four hour shifts.

Some jobs need to start 30 minutes to an hour before an Event begins. Other jobs need go past the closing time of an Event by an hour or more. So be sure your schedule includes these job times also.

The best way to do scheduling is to create a spreadsheet with dates, times and how many slots that need to be filled during each time slot.

For some Events it is easier to create a graphic with blocks of times associated with jobs that need to be done, with space to put the volunteer's name(s) under the time and job title.

When someone volunteers, write his or her name in the time slot for the job they are agreeing to help with at the Event.

You can either have spaces to put his or her contact information on the job spreadsheet or create a separate contact spreadsheet.

Either way you will want to have as many *"virtual"* ways to contact them as possible. Ask them for their phone number, text number and/or email as ways to contact them before and after the event.

When signing up a volunteer, be sure to ask if they have a cell phone or a SmartPhone that they will be bringing to the Event. Having that number can make communication at a large Event easier. And if they are late for checking in, you can try to contact them to find out why they haven't arrived yet.

Some Events use walkie-talkies to communicate with organizers and some volunteers. That can be a costly expense, but necessary in some cases. In some areas it is difficult to find a clear channel for walkie-talkies to use at the Event.

Renting them can be expensive, depending on the number needed. They also use batteries as their power source. Having enough rechargeable batteries for an annual Event is a challenge. Depending on the number of volunteers and Staff members, an Event rarely has enough walkie-talkies to supply everyone with one, leaving some people out of the communication loop.

With the rapidly changing communication technology, more and more Event organizers are able to use fewer walkie-talkies by connecting with their Staff and volunteers by using cell phones as the communication choice. This cuts down the use of batteries that are disposed of, and often guarantees faster and clearer communication between Staff and volunteers.

Since most cell phones run on rechargeable batteries, this is another way to have a more positive influence on the impact your Event has on the environment.

A week, or ten days before the Event, a reminder email needs to be sent out to all volunteers, to be sure they are still onboard. Remind them about their role in helping with the sustainable part of the Event.

In this email, make sure they know the time they should arrive and where they are to go to check-in when they arrive to get the training they will need for the job they will be doing.

If the Event has an entrance or ticket fee that is being waved for their volunteer participation, they will need to know how to provide proof to the people at the entrance that they are a volunteer and have a free pass to the Event. Usually a picture ID is required to be shown to get a free pass.

It is highly recommended that at this type of Event there is a list at the entrance with the names of all the volunteers on it. The ticket or fee collector will ask them to show a picture ID to get into the Event. Using this ID, their name will be found on the list, where it can be checked off and/or write the time of arrival there to show they arrived on time.

You could send them a free ticket by email that they would need to print out, but that isn't totally sustainable. But since paper tickets can be recycled, that would make it a bit better.

SmartPhones are becoming more and more mainstream, but not everyone has one yet. If a volunteer does have one, they could show the email they received designating them as a volunteer to the gatekeeper as another option.

The volunteer schedule needs to be posted at the check-in and training area. If someone doesn't show up, there needs to be a contingency plan in place to handle the tasks assigned to a missing volunteer.

Train Your Volunteers Well!

To ensure your Event is as successful in reaching its sustainable goal as possible, you need to be sure all your volunteers are well trained for the jobs they will be handling at the Event.

You can email out training information with the reminder email. But in most cases on site training will still be needed. On[sie training really works best for helping volunteers to totally understand the job they will be doing at the Event.

Having one or two people at the Event designated to do all the training is the best approach. This way the same information gets told to all the volunteers that show up.

If a group has volunteered and was given a free booth or information area, this is where the volunteers will come to get instruction. You could ask to have one or two of their people that plan on being there during the whole Event to do all of the training. Otherwise your organization will have to enlist someone to do this.

At the volunteer check-in area you will want to have photographs and a written list of the items that need to be sorted into each type of waste container.

Go over a map of the layout of the Event with every volunteer. Be sure they know where all the Waste Collection Stations are located. Be sure they clearly understand what types of waste that they will be responsible for collecting.

Show them the quickest route to where the waste that is removed from the public bins needs to go for its final pickup by the waste management service provider. Make sure each volunteer understands what type of waste will go into which of the large waste collection bins. Again, there should be very clear signage on all receptacles, small and large.

Be very, very clear about how even one plastic bag in the recycling or compost final collection receptacle can contaminate the whole container. This one mistake will WASTE everyone's efforts to make this a sustainable Event, as the waste in that container will end up in the landfill.

Be sure every volunteer knows where the biodegradable gloves are for them to wear during their shift. Demonstrate how to use the *"trash grabbers"* for sorting waste items that are in the wrong bin. Point out where they can clean up during and after their shift.

Volunteers who have a late shift and will be stationed at the end collection receptacles should be asked to take a good look into the containers and see if they can spot anything that was wrongly sorted. If there is, they must use the *"trash grabbers"* to move it to its proper container.

Volunteers who hang out as *"Bin Guardians"* at the end of the Event also need to offer helpful advice to the food and other vendors who are packing up to leave. This will help to assure sure they are sorting their waste properly and not just tossing it all into the landfill receptacle because they are tired and want to get out of the Event area quickly.

Job Related Items Waste Management Volunteers Will Need

Having boxes of biodegradable gloves for the sorters to wear when sorting is a must! Depending on how large and the timeframe of your event, volunteers can use dozens, or hundreds of gloves when sorting trash. Using biodegradable gloves, even if you do not have composting available at your Event means they took less energy and fewer nonrenewable resources to make than standard plastic gloves.

"Trash grabbers" are another handy item to have. You can buy an extended *"arm"* that has a gripper to handle messy trash items or are deep in the wrong type of waste container that need to be sorted out and moved to the proper waste container.

We found that Walgreens *"Gopher"* was very durable, reasonably priced and easy for everyone to use. But you can find similar items on TV, the Internet or other local stores.

You need to have a good number of these, more than one per time and job slot. They can get broken, and without one, a volunteer won't be very happy sorting the trash or unable to do the job as well as expected.

You need to have some type of name badge that designates these volunteers as *"Waste Monitor", "Bin Guardian", "Sustainable Volunteer", "Waste Rustler"* or some other designation that fits your Event. You don't need to have their names on the badges; in fact it would be best not to have the badges with individual names.

It is a nice touch if a specific organization or business is supplying all the volunteers to have the logo on this type of identification badge. This is another way for them to advertise to the public that they are Waste Wise conscious.

Ask them to turn in their badges after their shift ends, so each badge can be reused over and over again at this and future Events.

How To *"Reward"* Your Volunteers

We would like to think that helping the environment is reward enough, and for some volunteers it is.

But it sweetens the job of handling trash if they get a bit of something extra as a thank-you.

Rewards can be given out when a volunteer arrives or when they are ready to leave. If you are giving them T-shirts, they might want to wear that while doing their job.

If you have a water station and are using reusable beverage holders as a reward, give one of these to each volunteer at the beginning of their shift.

If you are rewarding them with food coupons that can only be used at the event, you definitely want them to have them during their shift or before the Event ends that day.

Commonwheel's Art Festival hands out $5.00 worth of food coupons to everyone who works a four-hour shift as a *"Bin Guardian"* or *"Waste Monitor"* or *"Waste Rustlers"* in the park. These food coupons must be used at the Art Festival at one of the food vendor's booths.

It is mandated that organizations holding any type of Event that involves sales in Manitou Springs' City Parks must collect and remit sales tax for all the vendors at the Event. Commonwheel's food vendors use the food coupons that the volunteers use to purchase food or beverages at their booths to pay their sales tax at the end of the Art Festival. That way the Commonwheel Art Festival can reimburse them without having to involve any actual cash transactions.

If you can afford to give volunteers a T-shirt, a reusable shopping bag or drink holder with the Event's logo printed on it, they get something useful and you get a bit of year-round advertising.

Whenever possible, it is a great benefit to offer the group bringing in a large number of volunteers a free booth. Here the group members can share what they have to offer the community all year round. If there is no extra booth space, you might offer some space at Event's Information Booth or Registration Table for their literature. Some might prefer to have their business card in the Registration packets. At the very least, their contact information should be shared on the Event's website.

At the Commonwheel's Art Festival, Transition Town Manitou Springs brings in many volunteers. A couple of their leaders help with the actual planning of the sustainable part of the art festival. Transition Town is given a free booth where the volunteers come to check in and get trained. At their booth they offer a great variety of information for the general public to learn more about what Transition Town and PermaCulture is all about.

In years past, they have had a massage therapist in the booth who offered massages for free or a donation to the group. People who came to the booth for their free massage became a captive audience to hear and learn about more about sustainable ways of approaching life while they waited for their turn or were seated in the massage chair.

2012 FESTIVAL SPONSORS

It takes many community sponsors to make this Art Festival successful. Their sense of community and support of the Arts is demonstrated in many ways. We appreciate their donations of time, labor and materials to make this Festival exciting, fun and sustainable. Thank you all for making the 2012 Commonwheel Artist Festival a huge SUCCESS!

PRESENTING SPONSOR:
The Gazette
gazette.com

MAJOR SPONSOR:
NEWS CHANNEL 13

WASTE-FREE FESTIVAL SPONSORS:
TRANSITION MANITOU SPRINGS
BESTWAY DISPOSAL

STAGE SPONSOR:

Special Thanks to the following businesses and individuals who donated their time and discounted or donated services to make this year's Festival successful.

Transition Town-Manitou Springs, Brian Fotz, Alicia Archibald, Bestway Disposal, Becky Elder, Blue Planet Earthscapes, Coreen Toll (M. S. Climate Protection Campaign), Gary Vigen (Poster Art), Robin Jones (Kids Booth), Masonic Lodge, Briarhurst Manor, Don Goede, CSFAC, Tajmo Alami, City of M. S. Parks Dept., Manitou Springs Chamber of Commerce, iManitou, Manitou Springs Police
And Commonwheel Artists Co-op together for all their volunteered time!

Zen Pixie Boyz will be your all weekend helping to keep the park clean, setting up tents and taking down Festival equipment. *Zen Pixie Kraftz* is a student run freelance marketing based crafted artists and goods. These items are made from outdated woods or acrylics and are hand turned on a lathe.
Students participate in the manufacturing process while learning small business optimization, 15% of the proceeds are used to reinvest in the business. Funds are used to support the students in their educational group pursuits and 15% is allocated to assist in the cost of MRF testing for the boyz.
As an incentive and display of hard work, top workers receive a salary. This program is designed to help the boyz gain work experience, and heirloom management skills and, most importantly, to support the Re-creative Consolidate Juvant Program.
We give back to the community one step at a time!
Zen Pixie Boyz help to keep the park clean, set-up & take-down tents and other Festival equipment.

Kids' Art Activities
NEW LOCATION
SE end of Park by Library's Book Sale

The Kids Art Activities Booth will feature wild fun measures to get to the top of your child's artistic need. Sun Robots and die gang are face painting, a fun looking workshop and other fun free arts and crafts. Kids will enjoy these art activities and interact with the family where no waivers provided.

Face Painting - South East end of Park
Half and whole faces painted using kid-friendly paints and glitter. (Donation requested.)

Gary Jones, "Magic Man" Balloon Artist
South Side of Stage

Giant Bubbles
Jim Jackson-MAT-Millian Art Theater
In Front of Stage

For 38 years Commonwheel Artists Co-op has brought Fine Arts and Crafts to the Pikes Peak Region.

In 2009 the Festival became a more "Sustainable" Event. 2009 & 2010 events were 66% & 2011 was 75% Waste Free. Our 2012 Festival Goal is to be a 85% Waste Free Event!

WAYS YOU CAN PARTICIPATE TO HELP GREEN THE FESTIVAL AND REACH OUR ZERO WASTE GOAL:

Utilize the Recycle and Compost Bins.
Read & Follow the Guidelines on How to Properly Dispose of Waste.
Buy ReUseable Bags to take home your art purchases.
Just $2.00 at the Information or Commonwheel Group Booth.

Bestway Disposal is donating all services for collecting and properly handling all types of waste generated at this Festival. They also donated the large and small bins to collect the waste including the containers for Recycle, Compost and Trash, plus all the wheeled carts that will help the Zeb Pike Boyz service the waste stations. Bestway will soon open a Material Recovery Facility (MRF) and has recently begun a commercial compost route. Bestway Disposal, a family owned local business, is committed to their community and helping to create a cleaner environment. Our Zero-Waste Major Sponsor.
The Bestway Disposal portalets use environmentally friendly components to reduce odor and clean hands. All paper products are created using recycled paper.

Transition Town Manitou is a local node in a grassroots international network of Transition Town initiatives, emerging spontaneously all over the planet as response to the growing crises of increasing environmental degradation, resource depletion, emerging energy scarcity and the fundamental invisibility of our economic system. All these ongoing events affect the stability and livability of our local communities. Transition Town Manitou aims to re-localize the material/economic base thereby to establishing an authentic resilience and sustainability within our community. This list of essential emphasis includes food, transportation, jobs and local economy, medicine and healthcare, appropriate handling of waste streams and energy production. In participating in the Commonwheel Festival in the role of Waste Removal Overseers/Bin Guardians, Transition Town Manitou will get to model appropriate waste stream removal and recycling practices as well as educate citizens as to their responsibility in creating authentic resilience and sustainability in their communities.

Coreen Toll (M. S. Climate Protection Campaign). The mission of the Manitou Springs Climate Protection Campaign is to encourage, facilitate and assist in the actualization of the goals and action steps outlined in the Manitou Springs Climate Action Plan adopted unanimously by the Manitou Springs city Council in June 2008. Part of our mission is to educate and motivate all members of our community to conserve energy and reduce their carbon footprint. www.manitouspringsclimate.org

Chapter 13

Chapter 13: Signage

Signs and programs are important elements for all types of Events. Creating the proper type of signage for any type of Event takes a bit of planning.

Weeks before the Event, you will need to decide what types of signs are absolutely necessary, and what materials will be used to create them.

Types Of Signs Needed

Signs thanking Sponsors and service providers who gave discounted services are particularly important at outdoor Events.

Large Events need maps of the Event's layout to help people navigate from the entrance to vendor booths and tables, stages, food areas and the restrooms.

Signs may be needed to direct people to areas with activities for children or to entertainment and presenting stages and all the other types of participants at an Event.

Outdoor Events often find there is no better solution to creating the many informational and gratitude signs that need to be made to handle these elements than having them laminated. Since most sponsors, entertainers, the layout of the event and schedules for the entertainment and presenters usually change from year to year; it is almost impossible to reuse these types of signs, and they can't be recycled.

But there are many other types of signs that can be reused from year to year. Signs with arrows pointing to restrooms or specific areas of the Event can be made in a way that they can be reused again and again. Be sure after the Event these signs get stored in a place they can easily be found again.

All types of Waste Wise Events will need signs that clearly designate all recycling, composting, and landfill containers and the liquid collection buckets in order to create a successful Sustainable Event.

This type of signage needs to specifically detail what type of waste goes into which container for the attendees to easily understand where to throw the type of waste they are holding.

Using images works better than just text signs. *But having a written list can also be helpful along side the images.*

You can create signage that can be used many times. Signs to educate participants about recycling, composting, water and energy conservation, and water stations *(when available)* need to placed throughout the venue and can be used at future Events.

Printed Programs

Many types of Events print up programs with schedules and locations of participants' booths, stages and conference rooms.

If your Event has a printed program, be sure to include information about the sustainability objectives you have for your Event and how you intend to meet them. Remind them to recycle the program when they no longer need it.

You can have fewer programs printed if you post the information on a website in a form that people can download to their SmartPhone or other device that they might bring with them, rather than needing a copy for everyone who attends.

You will still need to print some programs, but just not as many. Be sure you have well marked places for them to leave unwanted programs at the end of the Event so they can be recycled.

No Programs At The Commonwheel Art Festival

Many years ago, the Commonwheel Art Festival decided not to have any printed programs specifically printed to hand out at the Art Festival.

Commonwheel does print an informational flyer a month in advance of the art festival that gets distributed to motels, B&Bs, campgrounds, hotels and coffee shops around the area. This flyer includes a list of artists that will be attending, prizes offered in a drawing, food vendor menus, our sponsor's logos, thanks to volunteer groups, and a music schedule. This includes a caveat that any of this information is subject to change. We hold back a few of these to distribute at the Information Booth and a few well-trafficked places around the park.

Large laminated signs are placed in strategic places around the Park. These signs have the most up-to-date entertainment schedule and statements of our gratitude for our various sponsors. Plus, we will hang any reusable banners our sponsors provide near the stage area.

At the Art Festival's Information Booth we have a few large maps printed on paper that have all the artists names written in the booths where they can be found. We use these to direct art patrons to the artists they are searching for at the Art Festival. These maps are printed on paper with a high recycled content and get recycled after the festival ends.

The public never missed the up-to-date type of programs from the past. This saved us lots of time and money.

Although the laminated signs do end up in the landfill each year, thousands of pieces of paper never get printed upon, saving many trees and energy, so we believe that it is a reasonable trade-off for Commonwheel's Art Festival.

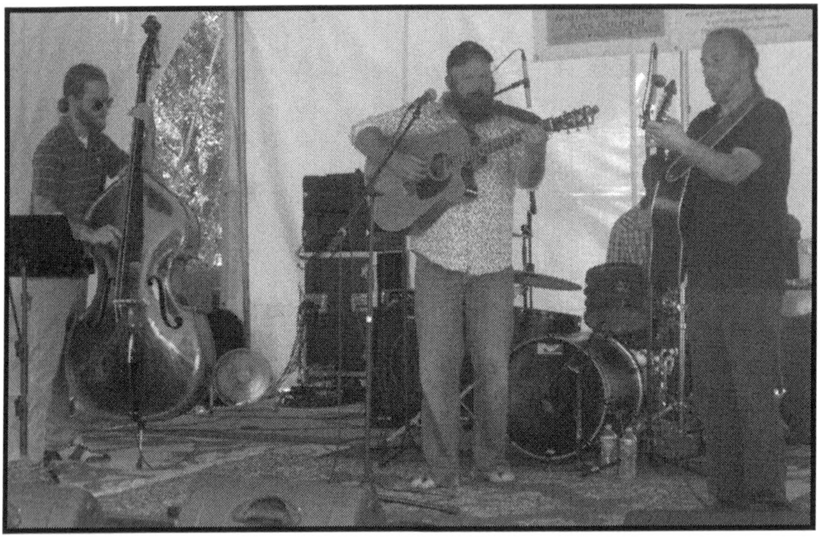

Chapter 14

Press Releases Before And After The Event

There are many ways to publicize an Event these days. Newspaper and magazine ads, posters, postcards, billboards, emails, flyers, newsletters, Facebook, Twitter, Pinterest, and word of mouth are the most used.

Social Media has become a very successful method to get the word out about an Event, but posters and paper ads still have a high appeal in some areas.

In a tourist area, if your event is a festival of some type the public can enjoy without much advance notice of it happening, having a small poster and/or printed flyer that can be used by the concierges at local hotels or given out to guests at other lodging establishments are usually very welcome. It helps them entice the guest to stay a bit longer. If it is an annual festival, sometimes guests will return the next year to purposefully attend that festival.

Before The Event

Whenever possible you want to include the information about your efforts to have a more sustainable Event. A Press Release can also include information about how the members of the public who will be attending your Event can participate and help in these efforts.

Sending out Press Releases before an Event can be used to share information about ways people in the community can participate in helping create a sustainable event and explain why you are doing this.

If you have a mailing list, you might want to try and transform it into an email list to save on postage and paper notices for future Events. This could take a few years to accomplish, but it will be worth the effort.

You will want to send out *"Save The Date"* information by email and posts on your website and Facebook page and other electronic means you use to minimize paper use.

Be sure the local Chamber of Commerce adds your Event to their online *"Calendar Of Events"*. It can help bring in many people in the surrounding area and visitors from afar that might not hear about it any other way.

Publicize your commitment to a sustainable Event in your outreach materials and in your communications with potential sponsors, funders, presenters, participants, and contractors.

If you have a program, be sure to include information in it about the sustainability objectives you have for your Event and how you intend to meet them.

Listed below are some things you may want to include in a Press Release before the Event.

- Suggest attendees bring their own reusable bags for purchases.
- Mention public transportation choices.
- If there will be a water station, suggest they bring reusable beverage containers.
- Describe ways that they can volunteer.
- Mention any type of reward or discount for people who participate in a big way.
- Explain the reasons you are doing this.
- Clearly state your sustainable goals for this year.
- Suggest ways groups can get involved.
- Ask them to repost on Facebook or reTweet about what you plan on doing.

If this is not your first year of hosting a sustainable Event, consider adding these types of informative items:
- Describe any new level or strategy you added this year.
- Share your past successes and relate them to your sustainable goals for this year.

Evaluation After The Event By Participants

You will want to ask the participants in your Event to help evaluate the sustainability aspects and how it impacted their participation.

Be sure everyone understands how important this is for you to keep improving the sustainable portion of your Event. Let them know how important their feedback is to you in order to create Events in the future that are even more sustainable.

You can add a paper survey in the *"Welcome"* packet for participants that you ask them to return at the end of the Event. Have an easy, well-marked place for them to drop it off at the close of the Event.

Better yet, you could create a survey using one of the many types of survey forms available on the web. A very popular survey is *"Survey Monkey"*, but many others also exist, either for free or for a small fee.

Keep your survey short. You should try to ask no more than six questions and, where appropriate, have a space for comments under each question.

To assure a better possibility of getting this feedback from your participants and attendees, immediately after the Event, send a link to the survey out in an email and ask for them to fill it out within the next few days.

Another way to let people know you want feedback from them is to add the link to a Facebook post, Tweet or on your website where you ask participants and attendees to fill out a survey after the Event.

However you chose to gather feedback about the sustainable portion of the Event, make sure you do it to help you understand what worked well and what needs improvement for the next Event.

After The Event Evaluate Measurable Successes

Immediately after the Event, take some time to calculate your successes.

Create a concise report highlighting the results of your sustainable efforts. Post it on the Event's website, send out a Press Release and share it in as many ways as possible.

This report should describe how much waste was recycled or composted instead of being sent to the landfill. You can talk about how much energy was saved or how many people used Public Transportation to arrive at the Event.

Evaluation of how much waste was diverted from the landfill at the Event is valuable information that can be used when determining how close to your goals you actually came. It will be invaluable information for Event organizers doing waste management planning for the same, or another Event, in the future.

If you did your pre-planning properly, you will have been able to have the information available by using the guidelines set out in your original planning.

Determining how much waste was diverted from the landfill is a high priority.

If you can't weigh it, but can take a good look before collection by your Waste Management Service, you can do an estimate using fractions, *i.e.,* 1/8 to Landfill; 1/2 composted; 3/8 recycled.

Or, if your Waste Management Service does have a way of measuring the waste by weight when it gets back to their location, you should ask to send a report to you as soon as possible after the Event ends.

If you know how many people came to the event using Public Transportation or carpooling or on a bike compared to the total number of attendees, celebrate that also.

If you used local produce for meals served, mention where it came from and what company you used to cater the Event.

If you had a water station, you should have an idea of how many gallons of water were served and then calculate how many plastic bottles were not needed when attendees refilled reusable containers.

If you had only local performers or speakers, mention how that helped the local economy and saved energy by their not having to travel very far to participate.

If you had participants stay in Green Motels, share the name and location of the lodging business.

If you conserved energy by using alternate energy sources, include this in your report.

Mention as many ways your Event was more sustainable from years past or other Events in the area.

Celebrate Your Success!

Any amount of waste diverted from the landfill, or any amount of energy saved is worth celebrating and sharing with your community!

Get excited about whatever level of sustainable success the Event achieves and share this information with the community.

Celebrate the many types of sustainable successes your Event experienced in as many ways as possible using Press Releases, Facebook, Twitter and emails.

Send thank you emails to your supporters, volunteers, groups involved, vendors, service companies and sponsors to share and celebrate how successful your Event was at diverting waste from landfill, supporting the local economy, saving fuel, etc.

Here are some ideas for what you may want to include in a follow up Press Release, email, Tweets or Facebook postings.

- Share the total amount of recyclables or compost that was collected.
- Explain how much waste was diverted from the landfill.
- Talk about how many people arrived at the Event in a carpool or on a bike or used public transportation.
- Express your gratitude to all your sponsors and vendors who gave discounted services.
- Mention how many volunteers helped create this Waste Wise Event.
- Thank the public for ways it participated and the many volunteers and any groups that worked to create a more sustainable Event.
- If you had a water station, estimate how many plastic bottles were not used by calculating how many gallons of water were give out to people using reusable containers.

Express Gratitude

It is extremely important to thank your sponsors both publicly and privately.

Be sure to send out letters, or emails afterwards to your sponsors, service companies, volunteers, government agencies and anyone else that helped make it success.

Include the sustainable success report in your thank you letters and emails.

Thank them profusely for their help and tell them that this type of success *"could not happen without YOU!"*

You can post on your website and Facebook page to tell the world how each Sponsor or volunteer group helped your Event reach its sustainable goal.

Some letters expressing gratitude are better when sent on paper, especially to your Major Sponsors. Just make sure you use a paper with a high content of recycled materials to print them upon.

And no matter how careful you are about limiting the amount of printed advertising items you create, you are sure to have a few left over.

It is a nice touch to include them in thank letters sent to your Major Sponsors, giving them proof of how their logos were used when you advertised the Event.

A photograph of signage or banners at the Event with their logo helps to impress upon them how many people saw they participated in this Waste Wise Event.

Commonwheel creates a Sponsor thank-you package that includes one flyer, postcard and/or poster that had our Major Sponsors' logos on them. We usually include an image of our Thank-You signs that are scattered around the park with their logo. These packages are hand delivered to their place of business with the thank-you letter attached. This serves the purpose of demonstrating how many people saw their logos in a variety of types of advertising promotional pieces, and makes them feel truly appreciated for their sponsorship.

A route is determined to include any other after art festival errands that need to be accomplished at the time the Sponsor Thank-you packets are to be distributed. Then one person usually drives to all the Major Sponsors places of business and takes care of as much other business, as possible in that one trip, such as returning rented items, for the most efficient use of a vehicle as possible.

If you don't want to hand out posters, just use a larger envelope to place the printed material in along with the thank-you letter. This type of *"Sponsor Thank-You"* packet can then be mailed.

Always be sure you have the proper name of the person at the sponsoring organization that you want to receive this bit of appreciation from your Event.

CYCLE RE
COMP
Compost -- No Trash!
PLEASE DUMP
LIQUID HERE
BEFORE
DISPOSING OF
YOUR CUP

Chapter 15

Lessons Learned

The first year Commonwheel Artists Co-op set out to create a more sustainable art festival, we had some very rough spots and unexpected challenges. Thankfully the ladies managing our efforts and our incredible volunteers made everything work well enough to create a 65% diversion rate for that first attempt.

We learned how very important it was to properly educate our volunteers on what we needed them to do and improve the signage at the public waste collection and final waste destination bins.

Pictorial Signage Works Best

Images, either drawings or photographs, on signs really help the public and Event volunteers better understand what type of waste goes into which container.

That first year we discovered just labeling the containers and only using text on signs to tell people what items went in which receptacles didn't work very well.

Photographs along with words describing the items that went into each type of bin worked much better the next year.

Placing signs in front of, or above, rather than on the lids of the containers worked even better.

Waste Monitor Duties

The first year, we had stationed *"Bin Guardians"* to monitor the disposal of items at each Waste Collection Station. This probably did help to increase the diversion rate, but it was a very boring job and took a lot of volunteers to do this. Almost every one of the volunteers suggested on their end of festival survey that we should look at doing it a bit differently the next year.

Every year since we have had teams of roving *"Bin Monitors"* armed with biodegradable gloves and *"trash grabbers"*. They go from one Waste Collection Station to another checking to see if there are waste items that have landed in the wrong container. If so, they use the *"trash grabbers"* or gloved hands to pull them out and transfer those items into the proper container. Many a lemon was saved from the trash and moved into compost. They also put the lemons resting atop the liquid collection buckets into the compost bins.

If the waste container was getting near full, they were expected to inform the people who had volunteered to empty the waste containers into the larger waste collection receptacles before a problem arose.

Commonwheel never actually asked the *"Bin Guardians"* to take on the task of educating the public; yet many of them did that as part of the job. One young man was a true comedian. You could see him talking to someone about to put a bit of waste in the landfill container that belonged elsewhere. He would have them laughing at whatever he was saying. They walked away smiling and feeling good about themselves rather than feeling they had been scolded or corrected.

Waste Containers

At the Commonwheel Art Festival we tried a couple of variations for waste containers during the first two years it became a Waste Wise festival.

Nothing looked as professional or worked as well as having the roll-off containers supplied by the waste management company the next years.

It is well worth the expense to use roll-off trash cans to handle the two or three types of waste you will be collecting at the Event.

Rogue Waste Containers

In various places on the outer edges of the city park where the Commonwheel Art Festival was held, were Manitou Springs City owned trash cans that were serviced by a different waste handling company and could not be removed.

This first year we didn't realize how many problems these *"rogue"* bins could cause us. People overfilled those trash cans with every type of waste possible. Vendors used them rather than trying to figure out where the waste they had should be deposited.

Some of our *"Bin Guardians"* tried to separate out recyclables, but it was a nasty job. Bees were also a problem at these *"rogue"* trash cans, making it a bit challenging to remove items.

The following years we covered those *"rogue"* trash cans that were staked into the ground with large plastic bags. We placed signs on them saying they were *"Out of Order"*.

Although this hasn't worked perfectly, it worked better than doing nothing with these immovable objects. Some people did ignore the signs, and a few even tore off the bags. But the majority of the visitors did respect the signs. Since they are located at exit areas of the park, we assume that most visitors either took their waste home with them, or brought it back into the park where they disposed of it in the proper provided containers.

Special Consideration For Food Vendors' Needs

Food vendors need to be provided with recyclable and compostable bins at, or very near their booths. It would be helpful for volunteer *"Bin Monitors"* to come by the food vendor's booths and empty these bins into the appropriate containers throughout the day.

We did not do this the first few years, hoping that the vendors would take the initiative to deposit their waste into the proper receptacles in a cooperative manner themselves. This ended up with a great deal of food waste that could have been composted, ending up in the landfill waste receptacle.

And at the end of any Event, food vendors can be very tired, and they may not have the energy, or proper mindset, to take the extra steps needed to figure out how to dispose of all the different types of waste generated from their food preparation in the appropriate bins.

We discovered that it was difficult for food vendors who don't have much extra help to get this right without a bit of coaxing and/or help from volunteers at the Art Festival.

In the future, we are considering providing compostable plastic bags for the food vendors. Food vendors have very few people working with them at outdoor Events. They often use plastic bags to collect all their waste. Even if they put the compostable waste into separate containers, they often bag it in plastic bags. Most prefer to do this than have open plastic buckets that can be easily transported and dumped into the compost bin.

Providing compostable bags could help avoid food vendors tossing loads of compostable items they have collected in plastic bags into trash bins. Some of our more conscientious *"Bin Monitors"* then pull out the bags and slit them open over the compostable bins and trash the plastic bags. Not a pleasant task.

End Of Day Caveat

The first year, we didn't schedule any volunteers to stay to monitor the waste area after the Art Festival ended. Each night we locked up all of the waste units and left.

But, the food vendors and artists still had to pack up and dispose of waste that had collected in their booths. Frustrated participants put trash in the *"rogue"* trash cans and the wrong large receptacles. Most just dumped everything into the small landfill collection receptacles that were unlocked.

The following years we made sure there was a volunteer posted near the large waste receptacles who could guide participants to which large or roll-off container to use for the end of day waste items.

Even if you think everyone has left the outdoor venue, don't lock all the waste receptacles. Leave at least one roll-off for each type of waste very obviously labeled and available, so participants can dispose of their waste items easily without contaminating the big containers. If possible, you will want to block access to the large waste receptacles or lock them, to avoid accidental contamination after dark.

A couple of times a volunteer actually crawled into the huge recycling collection receptacle to separate and remove plastic bags or bags full of compost or landfill waste. We thanked her heartily, but have tried to keep that from being a necessary task ever again.

Wildlife And Compost Or Any Food Waste

If your Event is held in an outdoor setting where wildlife roams, you need to consider how to handle this challenge. Be sure your security people are prepared for encounters with wildlife and remain a safe distance from any wildlife they encounter.

The park the Commonwheel Art Festival is held in has a bear problem. We had to figure out how to handle compost and recyclable items that smelled of food in a way that would not create a difficult situation for food vendors, security guards or the *"Bin Guardians"*.

We hire a security service to keep intruders of the human kind out of the park at night. Each year, they also have had to scare away bears from the large trash receptacles using lights and shouting at them. Luckily, our bears don't like to be challenged and leave quickly when confronted with bright lights combined with loud noises.

In other areas, raccoons or skunks in a city park can be a problem if the waste collection receptacles can't be secured properly with tight lids. And stray dogs can also be a challenge.

If an event is held in an area near forested land where mountain lions have been seen, that can create a very dangerous situation for someone walking in the waste collection area at night.

At night, the only people that should be in the area any outdoor event is held should be appointed or hired security guards. They need to be *"armed"* with bright lights and a horn. They can use these to frighten away wildlife around the waste collection bins. A can of Mace could be useful to protect themselves, if they encounter wildlife anywhere in the secured area after dark.

Disposing Of Compostable Items

The first couple of years, a volunteer had to transport the compostable items to a collection site located far north of our city.

During those first couple of years, a volunteer from the steering committee took the compost to her garage each night. She also volunteered to drive it to the compost facility. She was very determined to help make this a very sustainable Event.

Thankfully, and to the relief of this volunteer, the next year we found a Waste Management Sponsor that was able to handle the compost, as well as recyclables and the landfill waste. This also made it easier to judge how much waste was diverted from the local landfill.

It Gets Easier And Better Every Year

Each year, the *"Bin Guardians"* have seen an improvement in how well items get placed in their proper waste containers. After the close of the festival, in its fourth year, they said it was so easy they hardly had to pick any improperly placed items out of the containers at all.

Many of the same volunteers show up to do this job again and again, year after year.

When they see what a difference it actually makes, how little landfill trash is created compared to the compost and recycled items, it makes them feel proud to be a part of this endeavor.

Our Waste Diversion number has climbed a bit higher every year. In its fourth year, the Commonwheel Art Festival diverted 80% of the waste from the landfill.

Three weeks prior to the 2013 Art Festival, the park the Art Festival had been held in for 38 years, was flooded. Due to the logistical setback of having to relocate the festival, we only diverted 75% in its fifth year. Still we were very proud of that achievement.

Commonwheel Artists and Transition Town Manitou Springs will continue to work together in the future to create the most Waste Wise festival possible each year.

Whatever amount we divert, in coming years from the local landfill, we are happy knowing we have kept tons of waste materials out of our landfill and saved many trees and energy with by using and recycling items. Plus we have helped create healthier soil with the composted materials.

Chapter 16

Emails, Letters And Facebook Posts

You will need to send out many types of emails and letters to all your Event participants before and after the Event. In addition, you may want to post some of this information on your Event's Facebook page.

The emails and letters that need to be sent before a Waste Wise Event need to clearly define what all the vendors, suppliers and volunteers need to know so they can implement the proper actions. This information will allow them to fully participate in helping make the Event as sustainable as possible.

Emails to food vendors will be similar to ones sent to other vendors, but they will have some very important differences. Emails to food vendors need to include more specific type of information relating to service items, than the ones you will send to your other types of participants, such as presenters and non-food vendors.

In this chapter, you will find a simple description of the types of letters needed for different phases of the Waste Wise Event you are planning.

Sample Letters

Here is a link to a web page where you can find more detailed examples of these letters:
(http://www.howtoplanasustainableevent.com/sample-letters/)

Rather than starting from scratch, you are invited to use these sample letters as a starting point for what you need to communicate to food vendors, volunteers, sponsors and other types of participants regarding your Waste Wise Event.

There a few basic types of letters you will need to write each year.
- Invitation to groups and individuals to volunteer at the Event
- Letters to food vendors
- Letters to accepted participants
- Thank you letters to volunteers, sponsors and participants after the Event
- Success announcement

Some of these can be sent as an email and some can be posts on Facebook. Others will need to be printed on sustainable paper and sent as actual letters via the Post Office or hand-delivered.

Invitation To Volunteers

If your organization doesn't have enough in-house staff or volunteers to oversee all the parts of the waste management at your waste wise Event, you will need to reach out to your community in search of volunteers.

You will need to determine who within your organization can head up the project and be the main point person to contact all of the Event's participants, plus organize and schedule volunteers.

Or, perhaps you will you need to search for someone outside your organization to coordinate the whole effort.

Once you decide on which path to follow regarding the main person to handle this part of your Event, this will determine how your first few emails and Facebook posts will read.

If no one inside your organization will be heading up this project, put out a call for a *"sustainability coordinator"* for your Event. Be sure to explain how they will be compensated for this position. Let them know if you will be offering a monetary stipend or some other type of "reward" for doing this job. A free booth at the Event to promote their cause or business and access to all the Event's activities often is enough to get someone interested in doing this job.

If someone in your organization wants to head up this part of your Event, they will still need to put out a call for volunteers to act as *"Bin Monitors" or "Bin Guardians",* and *"Waste Rustlers"*. These can be two separate jobs, and can engage different types of groups or individuals.

Start by sending emails to groups that focus on different types of sustainable actions (gardening, renewable energy, recycling) in your community.

Post the same request on your Facebook page and ask people to Share that post.

You could make some phone calls to environmental cause leaders in your area to get suggestions from them about who to contact to help with this effort. Or, they just might be interested enough to join your Team.

Contact every University or College in your area. Ask them if they offer environmental, alternative energy or sustainability programs to discover if you could partner with them in some way. Mention that your organization is looking to find a motivated student to head up the program, or coordinate a group to volunteers at the Event. Ask if there would be a way for students to earn an educational credit at the school for their participation in a sustainable Event.

Each following year, it is important to continue to post a call for volunteers no matter who coordinates the effort. Members of the surrounding community need to hear about this opportunity and you may find some new energy to help take the program even farther than your original goal.

The Commonwheel Art Festival was very lucky. After the first round of emails and Facebook posts, two women responded who wanted to undertake all aspects of the Waste Wise program for that Art Festival. Their involvement during the first couple of years brought our efforts to the attention of Transition Town Manitou Springs and they took it over for the following years.

Commonwheel still puts up Facebook posts and sends out a few emails to help them gather in volunteers. Thankfully, a couple of leaders in that group have done most of coordination work to make it more successful and Waste Wise each year.

Letters To Accepted Food Vendors And Participants If Not Forewarned

If you decide to create a Waste Wise Event after sending out invitations or applications to possible participants, you will need to send a letter to them if they are accepted into the Event.

This letter or email needs to clearly state the guidelines they will need to follow to be participants at the Event. For food vendors this means you need to have a list of acceptable service items included in this notification to help them make a decision.

This letter or email must also contain a very clear "opt-out" clause in case they do not wish to comply with the requirements. Explain to them that if they do not want to follow the guidelines presented to them, they can opt-out for a full refund of any fees they have paid. Cleary state that if they wish to opt-out that they need to respond by email within seven days or less so you can find a replacement for them.

Make it a requirement that everyone who has been accepted respond by email to the letter very quickly, within seven days, to acknowledge that they understand the requirements, and are fully prepared to implement them.

This assures you that you have a good email address for them and that they will get all follow up emails relating to the Event that you need to send. Having them respond to the initial email makes it very difficult for them to claim ignorance of the guidelines, or that they didn't receive this important email.

Letters To Accepted Food Vendors And Participants If Forewarned

If you know you will be creating a Waste Wise Event before you send out the invitation or application for the Event, add the information in that item so that all potential participants can understand what they will need to do to properly participate in reaching your sustainable goals.

Be sure you ask them to include their email address when responding to this invitation or on their returned application.

Every year for future Events, the application or invitation needs to clearly state the guidelines and the goal for your sustainable Event in this item.

A follow up, very detailed email needs to be sent to everyone who will be participating at the Event. Cleary restate the guidelines, no matter how many times they have participated before.

If acceptance letters are sent out by mail, you will want to immediately send a follow up email to reconfirm that all participants understand that this will be a Waste Wise Event and what their role will be in making it successful.

Send out *"call to action"* emails to every type of participant, including presenters and entertainers.

Depending on what the goals of your Waste Wise Event are, you will want to clearly explain what type of actions each type of participant can implement in order to help the Event reach its sustainable goals.

Letters to food vendors will be the most detailed; and they will read quite different from ones sent to all other types of participants.

The follow up email to food vendors will also have an immediate *"call to action"* for them to implement.

You will want to make it a requirement for all food vendors to quickly respond to the email, within seven days, to acknowledge they completely understand all of the requirements, and are fully prepared to implement them.

Their quick response will confirm you have an email address that they frequently check. Thus assuring they will see follow up emails for the Event containing resources and ideas for how they can best participate to help the Event reach its sustainable goals.

If a food vendor doesn't respond quickly, make a phone call to let them know there is a problem that needs to be resolved immediately and their participation is in jeopardy.

Thank You Letters

After the Event is over, simple and different types of letters of gratitude need to be sent to volunteers, presenters, food vendors, sponsors and all other types of participants.

Most of these can be handled by using email, but sponsors probably need to be printed out and mailed to them. *(See chapter 14.)*

Post in Facebook how much you appreciated the public for properly disposing of waste items.

Even if you just recycled paper, let participants know in a Facebook post how their taking the time to drop off used programs or other paper they gathered at the Event in a recycle bin before leaving the Event site made it more sustainable.

Thank the sponsors, groups, coordinators and volunteers on Facebook for doing such a good job to make the Event as sustainable as possible that year.

Success Announcements

As soon as you have a good summary of how well the Event's sustainable goals were reached, announce it to the World in many ways.

This can be added to the thank-you letters that will be sent after the Event or it can be a separate email.

A summary of the amount of waste that was diverted from the landfill helps to awaken people's sense of pride in having helped create a sustainable Event. When possible, have a photograph to accompany your success announcements. This will really impress upon people's minds how they can make a difference by sorting waste and being mindful when disposing of all types of waste.

Use this information for Facebook posts after the Event is over. You can break it up into a post for each type of sustainable success you had.

Compile this information into an interesting story and send it to your local newspapers in a Press Release. Add thanks to the public and everyone who helped make the Event a sustainable Event to make it more personal for community members.

Chapter 17

Resources

This chapter contains a list of resources that everyone who is ready to create a sustainable Event can use to get started.

Always take time to make your own assessment regarding the vendors you are considering purchasing from to determine if they can meet your Event's standards for being truly sustainable.

When an Event controls what is used at it and/or what comes into it, then it is easier to control what goes out of it and where it ends up: landfill, compost pile or recycling center.

Sharing information about sustainability, and the reasons why you are creating a Waste Wise Event will help participants better understand the guidelines you have set up for them to follow.

Sharing resources for participants to easily find recyclable and compostable items will make it easier for everyone to comply with the Event's guidelines, and help the Event to more easily reach its sustainable goal.

The Internet if filled with information about sustainability. *The resources listed below are just a few starting points.* Many of these are ones that have been helpful to the Commonwheel Art Festival and other organizations that the author has worked with when creating a sustainable Event.

Use the below link to access a web page with all of these links that you can click on to easily access these resources.

http://www.howtoplanasustainableevent.com/sustainable-event-resources/

Recyclable And Compostable Service Ware

Compares vendors for biodegradable plastics (bioplastic).
http://www.pge.com/mybusiness/edusafety/training/pec/compostprogram/productlist.shtml

A free directory of composting facilities that can be found throughout North America.
http://www.findacomposter.com/

Resource for buying recyclable and compostable products. A "green" company that sells sustainable disposable products.
Eco-Products® that can be customized to build your brand with custom printed cups and EcoGrips®.
http://www.ecoproducts.com/

What to know before purchasing compostable service ware.
http://www.ecocycle.org/files/pdfs/Compostable_Food_Serviceware.pdf

Go green with Web Restaurant Store's eco-friendly plates and other flatware. Choose biodegradable bamboo flatware and dinnerware, or renewable, biodegradable silverware for a sustainable, trendy departure from regular disposable dinnerware! Perfect for elegant weddings or other catered events, these sturdy, chic wood and bamboo dinnerware products are a perfect way to go green.
http://www.webstaurantstore.com/459/green-biodegradable-dinnerware-and-renewable-wood-flatware.html

Resources to buy compostable service ware:
www.ecocycle.org
http://goodtogoware.com

EcoSafe facilitates building partnerships to resolve the challenges of source separation and collections using the best zero waste practices.
http://www.ecosafezerowaste.com/products/zero-waste-compostable-products.html
http://www.ecosafezerowaste.com/index.html

Sustainable Lodging.

This website offers a Green Product and Service Directory and a listing of eco-friendly lodging facilities.
It is the lodging industry's leading environmental news source.
www.greenlodgingnews.com

Eco-Labeling

Find Green Seal-certified hotels, green products and cleaning solutions. Green Seal uses science-based programs to help educate and empower consumers, purchasers, and companies to create a more sustainable world.
http://www.greenseal.org/

Find out what labels on products really mean at:
http://www.greenerchoices.org/eco-labels/

Seafood Watch shares articles about the Eco-friendly choice to make when choosing fish for entrée at an Event.
This website includes list for Safe and Low Mercury Fish.
http://www.montereybayaquarium.org/cr/seafoodwatch.aspx

Sustainable Organizations And Informative Websites

Green Meeting Industry Council inspires sustainability and community leadership. The site has more information on waste wise how to design sustainable meetings and Events. It includes information on sustainable Event standards.
www.greenmeetings.info

At Blue Ocean Institute, we seek to inspire a deeper connection with nature, in everyone touched by an ocean.
http://blueocean.org/

Discover wayst to go carbon neutral and fight climate change today at:
www.carbonfund.org

Visit "Sustainable Communities Online" for a more sustainable future at:
http://www.sustainable.org/

The Zero Waste Alliance (ZWA) has a clear and simple vision: a prosperous and inclusive future without waste. A future without waste and toxics is not just a dream; it's a necessity. Waste reduces the effectiveness of our businesses, increases pressures on the natural environment and harms the vitality of our communities. It does not have to be this way; waste is the result of a broken process. Fortunately, this is a process that can be fixed.
http://www.zerowaste.org/

The Cornell Waste Management Institute (CWMI) is a program in the Department of Crop and Soil Sciences in the College of Agriculture and Life Sciences at Cornell University. CWMI serves the public through research, outreach, training, and technical assistance, with a focus on organic residuals.
http://cwmi.css.cornell.edu/
http://cwmi.css.cornell.edu/factsheets.htm (composting)

Lane County Oregon helps Event organizers by sharing tips and suggestions for recycling.
http://www.lanecounty.org/departments/pw/wmd/recycle/pages/eventrecyclingbinsanddurables.aspx

Earth Friendly Promotional Products

There are dozens of companies where you can order Earth Friendly promotional items. Listed below are just a few places to get started. Do a Google search for the type of product you are looking for to expand your ability to find just the right product and provider who fits your product requirements.

4AllPromos has a really nice selection of reusable bags from the very simple to the very chic. You can personalize many types of products for giveaways with your company logo. There is something for every budget and every type of Event to be found here.
http://www.4allpromos.com/

Green Bag Promos offers eco-friendly tote bags with logo printing including wine totes, insulated bags and 100% biodegradable bamboo bags.
http://www.greenbagpromos.com/

1Bag at a Time® provides a bag that is clean, simple, and honest that can have a logo or message imprinted on it. They mostly do large quantity of bags for bigger events and promotions. It's a simple concept to reduce waste and create a cleaner, healthier life for each other, our planet and ourselves. We do it one bag at a time.
http://www.onebagatatime.com/

EcoFriendlyPromotions1's mission is to provide you with the best promotional products possible. This site is dedicated to environmentally friendly promotional products, where we work with premier suppliers and are dedicated to providing you with top quality promotional products to help ensure the success of your business. Feel free to browse though our vast array of eco-friendly products, and if you have any questions, just let us know. No matter what your budget is, we have a solution for you!
http://www.distributorcentral.com/websites/EcoFriendly Promotions1/

Branders.com has many biodegradable, organic, recycled and sustainable items that can have logos imprinted upon. A promotional "Garden Gems" paper planter is just one idea that can be found here.
http://www.branders.com/

Solar Stages
The best way to find a Solar Stage is to Google "solar stage, your town's name" to find a provider in your area. And yes, use the quotes to get the most specific results.

Alternative Power Productions simplifies the production process for events while lessening the environmental impact by integrating alternative energy with professional staging, and sound. We execute this by providing creative solutions, social integrity, and pioneering alternative energy production technology and most importantly optimal customer service.
http://www.altpproductions.com/index.html

Solar-powered-trailer-stage.
http://www.stage-tech.com/solar-powered-trailer-stage.html

Where To Find Volunteers
- Groups that need to do Community Service
- People working within your organization
- Groups focused on the Environment
- 4-year Colleges and Universities
- Friend and family Members
- Transition Town Chapters
- Girl and Boy Scout Troops
- Sierra Club Chapters
- Community Colleges
- Garden Clubs
- Hiking Clubs
- High Schools

(See Chapter 12 for more details on where to find and how to engage volunteers.)

Sample Letters
Check out this Website to access the following sample letters.

http://www.howtoplanasustainableevent.com/sample-letters/
- Invitation To Volunteers
- Letters to Food Vendors And Participants
- Thank You Letters
- Success Announcements

More Information On Sustainability
http://en.wikipedia.org/wiki/Sustainability

Chapter 18

In Conclusion

If you believe we can break away from relying so much on foreign oil and other unsustainable practices to create a healthier Environment, it is time to step up to help make that change a reality.

The Earth needs us to be more conscious about how we use its resources.

Landfills are filling up. Our rivers, lakes and oceans have been filled with items that will never breakdown and pollute the ground and water. The air has become polluted by gases escaping from landfills and exhaust from poorly run factories.

How will we explain to the future generations that we continued to purchase items that we did not recycle, reuse or compost, when that was an option for us? Will we tell them that we did it because it was *"good for the economy"*?

How will they understand this mindset when they can't farm the land, breathe the air or drink the water?

Take a moment now to consider how making an Event more sustainable will impact the future of many generations to come in very positive and measurable ways.

"Will those who come after us in a hundred or two hundred years, those for whom we are blazing a trail, will they remember and have a kind word for us?"

1899, Anton Chekov, Uncle Vanya, Act 1

It is not easy to change the way millions of people handle their trash items. But anyone can make a small start towards educating a few people at a time by creating a sustainable Event.

It only takes one person with an idea and the courage to ask for help from others to start the ball rolling.

"Each and every one of us can make changes in the way we live our lives and become part of the solution."

Al Gore

All types of small and large Events are usually filled with joy and get participants excited about what they are learning, seeing and/or doing.

Even an event as small as a family reunion, wedding or birthday party will create an unusual amount of waste that is gathered in one place. Larger events and festivals create huge amounts of waste. No matter the amount of waste created at these Events, it that can be channeled differently than in the past with a small amount of effort on the part of the Event Coordinator.

One way to educate and begin to show everyone how they can help is for indoor events and outdoor festivals all over the nation to make a change in how they handle waste.

Some types of Events must use disposable items to make that Event run smoothly. Using disposable items that are compostable or recyclable, gives every Event the opportunity to be more sustainable and more joyous for this planet called Earth that we live upon.

Using products or services that have a lesser impact on the environment, or that reduce negative effects on human health when compared with competing products or services that serve the same purpose helps to keep the Earth healthier and cleaner for future generations.

"Sometimes in the winds of change we find our direction."
Anonymous

Whether you are planning a small event such as a wedding or birthday party or a huge event or festival with thousands of participants, one or more of the strategies mentioned in this book can be implemented to make that Event more sustainable.

When planning any Event, take some time to establish sustainability policy or create a mission statement to share with everyone you want to enlist to help with this concept.

Ask for help from everyone you think might be onboard with this idea. Create a "Green Team" to help the Event reach its sustainable goal.

Break up the plan into sections that can be done by different individuals. Determine what needs to be done each day to reach the Event's sustainable goal, and then focus on getting that done.

Don't get overwhelmed by the big picture.
Focus on what you can do!

"Given the right circumstances, from no more than dreams, determination, and the liberty to try, quite ordinary people consistently do extraordinary things."
Dee W. Hock, Founder, Visa International and The Chaordic Alliance

Setting up a simple water station or using pitchers to serve beverages, such as ice tea, can make a huge difference. This will reduce the number of single-use plastic used at your Event. This simple step will save our precious resources and avoid sending more plastic to a landfill to decompose and pollute the land and air as they decompose.

Recycling has a very visual impact when comparing how many pounds of recycled materials are being diverted to a new life compared to the amount of trash in the containers headed to a landfill. It is easy to see how much more waste there would have been sent to a landfill without recycling items at the Event.

Every person who attends, and sees or hears about the success of the Event, will be prompted into thinking about ways they can make small changes in their life to create a more sustainable lifestyle and help protect our precious air, water and soil from becoming polluted.

"We are all caught in an inescapable network of mutuality, tied to a single garment of destiny. Whatever affects us in one way, directly affects all indirectly."

Martin Luther King, Jr.

It is almost guaranteed that after attending a sustainable, Waste Wise Event, at least one person who attended the Event will be inspired to help make another Event more sustainable.

And many others will become more aware of why recycling and/or composting is good for the Earth and be more mindful of how they dispose of their personal waste items at home and out in public.

A sense of pride will be instilled in all volunteers and organizers when they see how much waste can be diverted from the landfill.

By creating a Waste Wise, sustainable Event, you are taking a step for sustaining human life on a finite planet.

By doing this, you are investing in the future state for all humans in which resource-use can better meet human needs without undermining the sustainability of natural systems and the environment.

Being more aware of how we handle our limited resources now will help assure that future generations may also have their needs met.

The Earth will be grateful for you treading lightly upon Her and preserving the natural resources and gifts She has given to us.

And future generations will thank you for your consideration for helping to keep the air, water and soil free from pollution so they may enjoy a healthier life.

**"We do not inherit the Earth from our ancestors;
we borrow it from our children."**
Native American Proverb

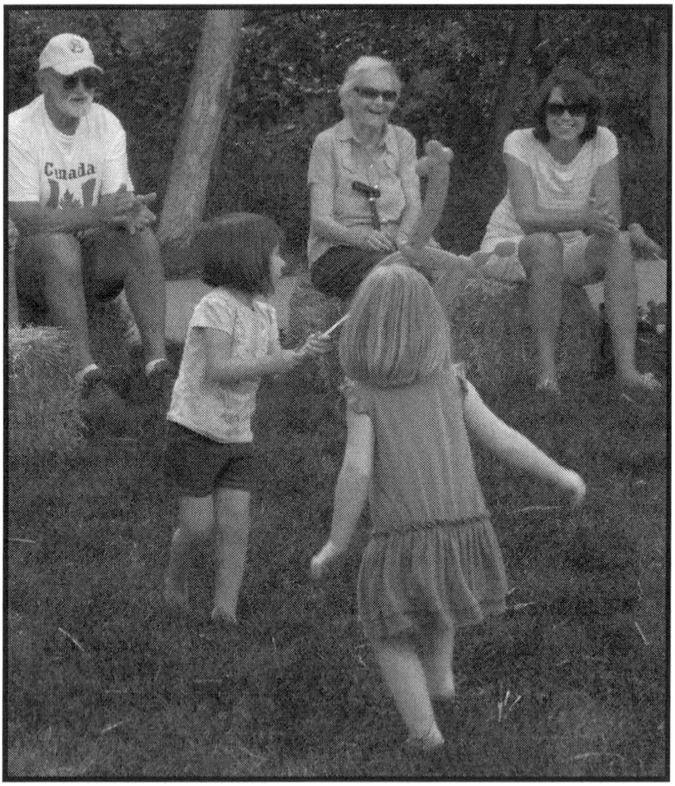
Canada

About The Author

Julia Wright lives in a small Colorado mountain town on a street that ends where a trail begins that goes to the top of Pikes Peak.

Manitou Springs is filled with holistic healers, artists and many people interested in creating a more sustainable lifestyle.

She has always been interested in ways to live gently on the planet. She grew up in a rural area of northern Illinois with parents who had a small garden and shopped at roadside farm stands all summer long. She loved playing in the out-of-doors then, and still choses hiking as her favorite way to celebrate the Earth's natural beauty.

Julia has been involved in coordinating the Commonwheel Artists Co-op's Labor Day Art Festival since 1976 when she joined the Co-op. It has grown from a tiny Art Festival to a regionally renowned and hugely successful Festival that celebrated its 40th year in 2014.

In 2009 she suggested to the Festival committee that they should look at creating a more sustainable Art Festival. They agreed, but it took many community members outside of Commonwheel to make this happen. The City of Manitou Springs, Commonwheel Artists and Julia have been very involved with creating a more sustainable world in many ways.

Recently Julia, and Commonwheel have been recognized by Manitou Springs City Council and Manitou Springs Art Council for her work in the art community and aiding in reaching the sustainable goals set by the City.

This book came about when she realized how many people are interested in learning ways to make Events they coordinate or participate in more sustainable.

Most books she found offered very complicated and had expensive ideas for how to create a more sustainable Event. This book is very user-friendly and invites people to take one simple step, then another, to make a change in the way an Event handles waste, so as to not be overwhelmed.

Julia began her artistic career in High School where she was deeply involved in the behind the scenes areas of theatrical productions. Her love of theater and creating sets morphed into a more craft oriented world when she started doing macramé using found objects and driftwood. She added woven images into the jute frames and began working with feathers in 1978 when she created her first meditation mandala.

She was introduced to essential oils over 19 years ago when recovering from a bad car accident and had a minor concussion. She has used them for many purposes such as healing her body and mind and as (non-polluting) cleaning solutions. Her first book was inspired when searching for a way to share her knowledge of how essential oils can aid in naturally keeping a person and our planet healthy. Look for *Discover Essential Oils For Optimum Health* on Amazon or her website: www. DiscoverEssentialOilsForOptimumHealth.com.

After the car accident, she began creating feather masks and jewelry. Each *FantaFaces* mask has a character all its own and sparks an instant transformation when someone places one on their face. She often incorporates found objects (recycling) in her feather pins and pendants. Come play at http://www.fantafaces.com.

In 2013, the Waldo Canyon Fire turned many acres of land above Manitou Springs into hydrophobic soil. This put Manitou Springs at very high risk for flooding. Julia had experienced flooding at her home in 1997. And in 1999, Manitou Springs experienced floodwaters that came down Williams Canyon; one of the major watersheds from the area the fire had destroyed.

When she realized people were not taking the flooding threat as seriously as they should, she found her photographs from the 1999 flood, and wrote *Lessons From Past Floods: Destruction, Restoration and Preparation* in hopes the town would be more prepared in case of another flood.

Unfortunately, no one, including Julia, was prepared for what happened on August 9, 2013 when muddy, debris filled waters raged down Williams Canyon and into Manitou Springs.

After the waters receded, many basements, including Commonwheel's, were filled with a couple feet of this nasty smelling and sticky mud and debris. *(Yes, a new addition of her "Flood" book needs to be written, but it is still too close to the incident to write about it.)*

The floodwaters also raged through the park where the Art Festival had been held for the past 38 years. Julia, with lots of help from the community and other members, relocated the Commonwheel Artists 30th Annual Labor Day Art Festival to another park in Manitou Springs in less than three weeks. But that is another story . . .

Julia has also helped other people get published on Kindle and Amazon's CreateSpace. Plus she has published a number of books on Kindle herself. Find out how she could help you get published, or discover more books she has written and those that will be coming out in the near future at: www.HieroGraphicsBooksLLC.com.

View of Manitou Springs from high up in Williams Canyon before the flood in 2013.

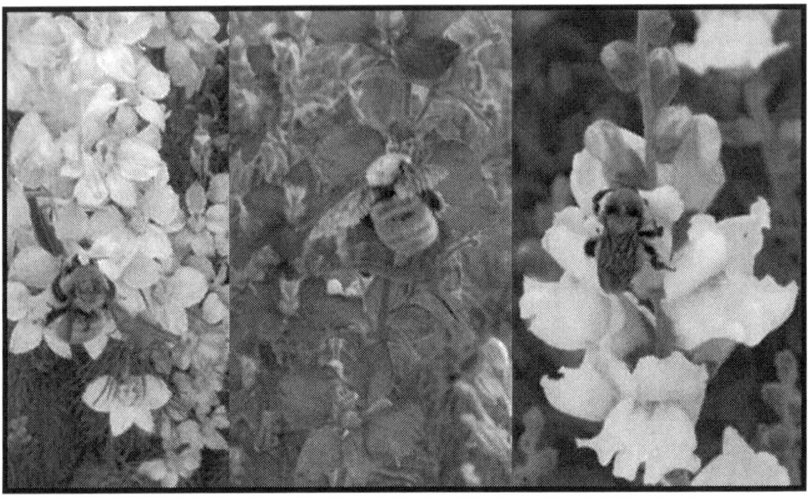

Notes

Notes

Notes

Printed in Great Britain
by Amazon